What People Are Saying About
Carlos A. Rodríguez and *Drop the Stones*...

"Carlos Rodríguez writes with grace, and about grace. His book is a stunning invitation to look into the face of Jesus and see that the only One who had any right to throw a stone had no desire. We see in Jesus that the closer we are to God, the less we should want to throw stones at other people. This is nothing short of a call to reimagine Christianity as a faith that fascinates the world with love."

—*Shane Claiborne*
Author and activist

"Too many Christian authors today pen books bursting with lifeless prose, syrupy self-help advice, and pat answers to deep questions. Thankfully, *Drop the Stones* is not one of those books. In these pages, you'll find practical principles laced with the passion of an author who lives what he believes. You'll encounter stories of hope and transformation that will awaken dreams you didn't know you had. And if you stop to listen, you'll hear the Spirit speaking. I couldn't be more grateful for this book!"

—*Jonathan Merritt*
Contributing writer, The Atlantic
Author, Learning to Speak God from Scratch

"I have a new favorite book and a new favorite writer. This book overflows with wisdom, honesty, joy, insight, and Jesus. It will fill your heart, right after kicking you in the backside. After you read it, I hope you'll buy a dozen copies to give to all your friends, because we all need *Drop the Stones*."

—*Brian D. McLaren*
Author, The Great Spiritual Migration

"When a chorus of judgement goes up in many corners of the church, Carlos Rodríguez is singing a different song. He's not saying he's hitting all the notes right, but his ear has been captured by another melody altogether—the sweet refrain of divine compassion. Will you harmonize with grace and truth? *Drop the Stones* gives us the anointed vocal warmup to do just that. Pick this up and start practicing today—better yet, get all your friends reading it too and become a new kind of choir!"

—Mike Morrell
Writer and facilitator, mikemorrell.org
Co-author with Fr. Richard Rohr, *The Divine Dance: The Trinity and Your Transformation*

"Carlos Rodríguez writes with honesty and urgency as he calls the church to live up to its high calling to embody the love of Jesus. Drawing on his own pastoral experience, and touching on contemporary issues from ISIS to mass incarceration, *Drop the Stones* invites followers of Jesus to let go of culture war clichés and do the hard things of Jesus-styled love."

—Brian Zahnd
Pastor, Word of Life Church, St. Joseph, MO
Author, *Sinners in the Hands of a Loving God* and *A Farewell to Mars*

"Carlos Rodríguez has written a timely masterpiece on God's boundless, pursuing love of unworthy offenders and those who judge them. *Drop the Stones* is a bold, prophetic call to renounce judgment and say 'yes' to Jesus' irresistible invitation to embrace sinners, beginning with ourselves. Carlos's honesty and vulnerability disarm the reader, inspiring confession, conversion, and a full-on joining to Jesus' movement of world-transforming love. Read this and join up with Jesus to love this broken world into God's kingdom."

—Bob Ekblad
Director, Tierra Nueva and The People's Seminary
Author, *Reading the Bible with the Damned, A New Christian Manifesto,* and *The Beautiful Gate: Enter Jesus' Global Liberation Movement*

"In *Drop the Stones*, Carlos Rodríguez has, with candid and culturally relevant language, confronted the practical atheist in every professing Christian. The latent Pharisee in me was exposed more than once as I read the powerful and poignant stories contained within these pages. Thank you, Carlos, for 're-minding' us with the mind of a loving and nonjudgmental Christ."

—*Dr. Randall Worley*
Author, *Brush Strokes of Grace* and *Wandering and Wondering*

"*Drop the Stones* is a journey of crippling pain, loss, and the search for redemption. Each chapter chronicles the sacred and humiliating path toward wholeness and deep integration. This book is a holy witness to the never-ending revelation of God's mercy, always reminding us that Christ's love is greater than our sin. I pray this work will undo the years of self-righteousness and false humility that religion has taught, while ushering all of us into a new-found recognition of the abundant grace available in Christ Jesus."

—*William Matthews III*
Artist and Advocate

"Having been a student of Jesus and Scripture for nearly thirty years, I have come to the conclusion that the more conservative our belief in Scripture—that is, the more deeply we believe that every word of it is true—the more liberal we will be in the way that we love. The more faithfully we walk the narrow path of Jesus, the broader our embrace of fellow sinners will be. It is not in spite of our faith in Jesus that we love, listen to, and learn from those who do not share our faith, but precisely because of it. In a time when Christianity is often confused with separation, judgment, scorn, and exclusiveness, books like *Drop the Stones* are a needed correction, not to mention a welcome breath of fresh air. May we listen carefully to Carlos's words. More importantly, may we order our lives around them."

—*Scott Sauls*
Senior pastor, Christ Presbyterian Church, Nashville, TN
Author, *Jesus Outside the Lines*, *Befriend*, and *From Weakness to Strength*

"Carlos Rodríguez shares powerful stories of transformation we all need to hear. He provides inspiration for what's truly possible when we respond to the Holy Spirit. You'll find great encouragement through these pages."

—*Margaret Feinberg*
Author, *Fight Back with Joy*

"In an age in which the church is known more for what it stands against than what it stands for, *Drop the Stones* gives a much-needed call for us to walk in the love of Christ toward all people. I have had the privilege of working with Carlos for a number of years. I have walked through some of the experiences that he shares so honestly about and I have seen the love of God transform him and his family. I love his honesty, his transparency, and his ability to provoke religious thinking, but most of all I love his calling to activate all of us to be more like Jesus. I encourage you to read this book. You'll probably find some stones in your hands that you need to drop, as I did!"

—*Ash Smith*
Lead Pastor, Catch the Fire Raleigh-Durham

"*Drop the Stones* is a heart-wrenching, personal, funny, and terrifying look into the judgment toward others each of us harbors in our own soul. I'll be insisting all my friends read this!"

—*Carl Medearis*
Author, *Muslims, Christians, and Jesus*

"*Drop the Stones* is beautifully written and easy to read! Carlos has such a non-dualistic way of drawing on wisdom from such a broad spectrum of the body of Christ. Proof that he himself dropped the stones a long time ago."

—*Jason Upton*
Christian singer/songwriter

DROP
THE
STONES

CARLOS A. RODRÍGUEZ

WHITAKER
HOUSE

DROP THE STONES:
When Love Reaches the Unlovable

carlos@happysonship.com
Happysonship.com

ISBN: 978-1-62911-908-3
eBook ISBN: 978-1-62911-909-0
Printed in the United States of America
© 2017 by Carlos A. Rodríguez

Whitaker House
1030 Hunt Valley Circle
New Kensington, PA 15068
www.whitakerhouse.com

Library of Congress Cataloging-in-Publication Data (Pending)

1 2 3 4 5 6 7 8 9 10 11 🅦 24 23 22 21 20 19 18 17

To Catherine,

You are the gorgeous embodiment of the message I'm trying to convey
(and still trying to learn).
Thank you for loving me despite me. Te amo.

Michael,
Keep sharing
grace + truth.
Hugs.

Rev. 3:21

CONTENTS

FOREWORD

The churches I grew up in were more colorful than the Bible stories told via Flannelgraph in their back rooms, and the people as colorful as any characters in the Old Testament. The highlight of our church year was the state camp meeting in the summer, when all the churches in our region would gather to sing and shout and pray and sweat in the North Carolina July heat. The visiting evangelists, like professional wrestlers, all seemed to me to have their own respective "finishing maneuver." My favorite was the one who, when he gave the altar invitation, would actually lay his Bible on people, rather than his hands, causing them to "fall out" under the power of the Holy Spirit. Sometimes he would actually throw the Bible at people, saying, "Receive the glory!" And bam! They were on the floor.

The night I took my little Baptist high school girlfriend to camp meeting, the evangelist called out another preacher sitting in the front row. Then he did what I dubbed the "seven-dipper" on him: after touching him with his Bible, and the inevitable fall to the floor, he had the ushers bring him staggering back to his feet, then down he went—*seven more times!* Each time the evangelist touched that preacher, he would go "out in the Spirit" again and again. As you might imagine, it was an interesting ride home with my girlfriend in my old, gray Mustang.

I didn't really question the validity of those experiences then, but I mostly felt like an outsider to them—like the electricity everybody else was feeling when the Bible touched them was somehow unavailable to me. I waited in many a prayer line at that altar, the floor looking like a Civil War battlefield with bodies strewn all around—yet I was the one guy still standing upright. At the time, I assumed I was simply less spiritual than everybody else.

Then you blink and suddenly it is twenty years later, and I'm reading the scorching-hot book by Carlos Rodríguez that you hold in your hands, and lo and behold, I finally got my blessing. This book knocked me out flat on my back under its power. I'm writing this sitting up under a big June Oklahoma sky, but my soul is still on the mat from finishing it. Have mercy.

Carlos just gets the gospel. He gets it in a revelatory, intuitive way; he gets it in a Jeremiah fire-shut-up-in-my-bones way, in a God-in-the-dirt-underneath-your-fingernails way. The writing is lyrical, potent, human, and vulnerable…like the best kind of hip-hop, equal parts swagger and soul-baring. If Kendrick Lamar went to seminary and wrote an album full of bars about the gospel, I'm pretty sure this is what it would sound like.

I was sitting on my couch weeping and rejoicing only a few pages in. I found myself in the story of John 8 that Carlos narrates for us—inside of the story, and on all sides of the story. I experienced rapture, ecstasy, and bliss at the sheer unadulterated power of the gospel that crackles through these pages. It threw me to the floor; it stood me back up; and it sent me crashing down all over again.

Of all the young Christian leaders I know, Carlos is the one who inspires me the most. He has a style that is entirely his own, full of wisdom and passion and wit and fire. You get to sit close enough for the preacher to spit on you in this tent revival. Don't be afraid. There's nothing but mercy flaming red inside of him. Let the man preach. He's got a big, bold message of love, and he's preaching grace as hot as if it were fire and brimstone.

Drop the Stones is pure grace, uncaged, wild, ferocious, and free—as you will be if you let these words have their way with you, all the way to the end.

To all the pages ahead, I call back my response from the front row: *Glory*, and *Hallelujah*, and *thank You, Jesus!*

Preach, preacher. The whole world needs to listen to you.

The good news has never sounded any better than it sounds through your voice.

—*Jonathan Martin*
Author, *How to Survive a Shipwreck* and *Help Is on the Way*
Teaching pastor, Sanctuary Church, Tulsa, OK

INTRODUCTION

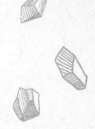

This is all about the woman who was caught in the act of adultery (us), the religious men that wanted to kill her (us), and the Christ who saved her (us).

The story that drives us is found in John 8:2–11. These verses almost didn't make it into the Gospel narrative. A few Bible versions don't even carry this holy moment. But I'm so glad the church fathers recognized the need for every generation to be exposed to this, especially ours.

In the next few pages you will read anecdotes, parables, and invitations, all filtered through this one statement, *"Let him who is without sin among you be the first to throw a stone"* (John 8:7). I wrote this book not because I wanted to fill your head with my conclusion about it but rather to welcome you into a conversation. Some of the topics will be controversial and others will seem unnecessary. However (and I'm telling you this secret because you're reading the introduction and most people don't read this) all I want you to do is think about it; to consider a different perspective; and to discuss it with your parents or your spouse or your enemies.

If you get annoyed with me, push through. If you love what I'm saying, tell every single human being on Twitter. And if you find yourself rediscovering the love of God for yourself and others, then we're all winners.

I like you already.

Let's keep talking.

Early in the morning he came again to the temple. All the people came to him, and he sat down and taught them. The scribes and the Pharisees brought a woman who had been caught in adultery, and placing her in the midst they said to him, "Teacher, this woman has been caught in the act of adultery. Now in the Law, Moses commanded us to stone such women. So what do you say?" This they said to test him, that they might have some charge to bring against him. Jesus bent down and wrote with his finger on the ground. And as they continued to ask him, he stood up and said to them, "Let him who is without sin among you be the first to throw a stone at her." And once more he bent down and wrote on the ground. But when they heard it, they went away one by one, beginning with the older ones, and Jesus was left alone with the woman standing before him. Jesus stood up and said to her, "Woman, where are they? Has no one condemned you?" She said, "No one, Lord." And Jesus said, "Neither do I condemn you; go, and from now on sin no more."

(John 8:2–11)

ACT 1

THE MEN

So, are we done with this bastard?" said the bearded man after spitting heavy on the floor. A deafening "Aye!" was the undivided response from the holy rascals gathered secretly in the dark. A common goal had brought them together. Yes, they were usually repulsed by each other: scribes, Pharisees, and teachers of the Law. But the one guy and his twelve morons had inspired unity within their ranks. In just a few months, the nuances of their disagreements were dissipated by the offensive and unlawful revolt initiated by the carpenter's son. Healings and feedings and stories about "good" Samaritans were more than enough to prove that this fad needed to be stopped. The new kid needed correction, and they were all so good at correcting.

"He's from freaking Nazareth!" said a young apprentice.

"Not just that, he never trained with any of us," replied his mentor.

"We keep losing money, people, influence…," added Caiaphas the High Priest. "I'm so done with this drunk rabbi and his crowd of misfits!"

They all nodded in agreement.

"Well," uttered a man standing to the left, "at least he's good with magic tricks!"

They all laughed for a second, but it only lasted a second. There was no space for joy in this gathering (not like there was ever space for joy in any of their gatherings). They all passionately hated the self-proclaimed Messiah; the way he blessed the children, the way he talked about God, the way he moved among the masses. They could not stand how close he got to those filthy trespassers and how little he allowed the Sanhedrin to guide him.

And they agreed with religious fervor that it was God's will to eliminate him.

Funny how all things work together for the good.

"But how?" asked the young apprentice. "The people seem to love him."

"Because he's one of them!" replied a few scholars simultaneously, pointing to the city.

Then, in a rare moment of silence, a short man walked up to the front of the mob. His slow pace and the way he rubbed his chin signified deep thought. "I have a simple plan, my brothers," he said without hurrying. "It's a godly, simple plan."

He began to talk about a woman he suspected of a grave sin and the opportunity to catch her in the act of adultery. He gave details about her exploits, and he was so sure of himself, that he had to control the excessive saliva leaking out the side of his mouth.

"What does that have to do with Yeshua?" asked Caiaphas. "What does that have to do with Yeshua?!"

"Ha!" said the short man beaming. "You all know this as well as I do. According to God's Law, when someone is caught in adultery, they must be stoned. Moses would understand this opportunity and I interpret it to be legitimate."

That's when their bushy eyebrows arched high as they exchanged surprised looks.

"Continue," said Caiaphas, slowly.

"We all know it's the woman who seduces anyways, right? And we all know that the boy from Nazareth is seducing Israel. What if we get them both?" concluded the stout man convincingly.

"Aye!" shouted the fevered crowd.

"Aye!" they shouted again.

1

BENEFITS OF STONING

"You can safely assume you've created God in your own image when it turns out that God hates all the same people you do."[1]
—*Anne Lamott*

I hate sexual predators. But when I'm sharing about God's love I try my best to pretend that I love them too. You know that verse? *Hate the sin but love the sinner.* Well, it's not a Bible verse at all, but my Christianity was built on it.

In 2008 I was invited to speak to the inmates in the maximum-security prison of Arecibo, Puerto Rico, so I was exposed to a few of these perverts. And prison is not the place to be when you're preaching something you don't believe in. However, my ability to spout spiritual hypocrisy was unmatched, and more than eighty convicts were exposed to the full repertoire. They were all dressed in bright orange jumpsuits while sitting uncomfortably in the hottest jail ward. I'm pretty sure this is the closest I've ever been to Hades.

But thank God that there were strict rules to protect visiting preachers:

1. No touching the prisoners.
2. No stories that would instigate a reaction.

3. No crossing the imaginary line created by the two guards on opposite sides of the front row holding massive rifles.

This was my second visit to this jail and this is the second time I have written about this story. I finished my first book *Simply Sonship* sharing about what happened that night. And although my retelling here is from a similar perspective, I write it because it is necessary for our conversation.

You see, that day I thought I was fulfilling my Christian duty both as a local church pastor and as a wannabe evangelist. But the truth is, I was there so I could impress people by telling them that I had been there. The incarcerated were not my priority; I was interested in their salvation only because of how it would make me look and feel. If I could get at least ten of them to raise their hands while I made the invitation to say "yes" to Jesus, then I would be validated and worthy of my salary and my calling.

More importantly, I could write a book about how people should be visiting the incarcerated and getting them to say "yes" to Jesus.

Welcome to Drop the Stones.

I know, I know, I was in that prison for selfish reasons on that humid-to-hell evening, and yet the most selfless One met me there. That's just how He is.

I was teaching good theology (according to my good theology), and while presenting the case for Christ with humor and conviction, I was passionate in my delivery and sure of a good outcome (according to my mom and my super-healthy self-esteem).

However, in the middle of my sermon, God interrupted me.

I knew it was Him because He was wiser and nicer than me. It was that still small voice that can almost be annoying. And He said to me, as clear as anything I have ever heard, "Tell the men who have sexually abused their daughters that I forgive them."

Absolutely not.

Of course I wouldn't do that.

I had a sermon to preach. I had rules to obey. I had a reputation to protect; yet I knew He said it. I can't tell you how I knew for sure it was God; I just knew for sure that it was Him. Maybe, despite the prideful motivations that brought me to that prison, God still loved me, still believed in me. Or maybe, just maybe, even though I was being an ass, God had a message for the men in front of me and He would use an ass, once again, to deliver His holy words.

A second time I heard Him say, "Carlos, tell the men who have sexually abused their daughters that I forgive them."

Trust me, gracious reader, everything in me was battling this madness. My mouth kept moving in the rhythms of the preaching but my brain was firing arguments like a sniper to the heavens. You know that feeling? When you're speaking out loud to others but having a full-on conversation in your mind about something else?

There's no way I'm going to say that, God! I thought, over and over again. *And even if I say it, if any of these locos respond to it, they will die!* And that, right there, was a legitimate protest, so I held on to it.

There's a gang in Puerto Rico called Los Ñetas, and when they find a man who has sexually abused a child, they will cut him to pieces and flush him down the toilet.

Literally.

That got me thinking, *Satan must be tricking me! There is no wisdom in this insanity. I rebuke you in Jesus' name!*

But then, God spoke to me again and I knew somebody had to stop Him.

What I thought next was the ultimate counterargument for denying the Lord's request: *Father, I don't think You should forgive people who have sexually abused their daughters anyway!*

To be clear, I still don't.

But I'm not God.

Neither are you.

And that right there is the good news.

It's been nine years since that day and I'm still uncomfortable with the memory and the re-telling of this event. I am aware that many of the people who are reading these pages were sexually abused themselves. There are no words to describe the pain and turmoil produced by such robbery of innocence. I can't even imagine how unfair it must feel. And one of the reasons I was so against saying what God was telling me to say was because I pictured my nieces and felt such anger in the moment that I wanted to punch these men, not heal them.

Yet it was reckless mercy that arrested me; irrational love that took over; and in a great moment of weakness, I agreed with God's version of the gospel.

Time seemed to stop as I paused the ramblings of my sermon and said decisively into the pungent microphone, "If you have sexually abused your daughters, I want you to know…that God the Father forgives you."

Yes, I told the men in front of me that they were exonerated of the vilest act. So the room went quiet, the air got thicker and I fully experienced the words of Richard Rohr: "Before the truth 'sets you free,' it tends to make you miserable."[2]

Yet for some reason, after I heard myself say the statement out loud, I began to believe it. I believed it with all of my heart. I believed it so much that the stares of the guards, the bewilderment in my team's faces, and the discomfort of the heat and humidity did not prevent me from saying it with spitfire compassion again: "If you have sexually abused your daughters, I want you to know that God the Father…forgives…you!"

In that moment, a man seated in the second row to my right stood up as if he were about to collapse, and shouted with all his might, "¡Maria! ¡Maria! ¡Perdóname!"

Maria was his daughter's name.

Perdóname is "forgive me" in Spanish.

And that was the moment I first met the Jesus of John 8.

I had good, ethical, biblical grounds to stone that man—maybe not in the flesh but at least in my heart. But as I saw the liquid repentance streaming down his face, I remembered my own sin, and I was glad that the God who saved me was not a monster like me, or him.

The room took in a deep breath of grace as the men who were sitting next to the abusive father stretched out their hands, squeezed his shoulders tight, and began to cry.

God was writing a message on the grey walls of this facility. I never had to say it out loud but we all heard it clearly: "If there's forgiveness for *that* sin, then surely there's forgiveness for mine."

I know they received that message because, one by one, almost every single one of these convicts became convicted. Some of them pounded the floor as they fell on their knees while others stretched out their arms as far up as humanly possible. The guards were so stunned that I looked back to the guys who were with me and, with a nod of my head, whispered, "Let's go in."

We crossed the invisible line of protection and began to hug our brothers. I don't know who was crying harder, but in the midst of the chaos, another man stood up in the last row and began to beg God for forgiveness. He was shouting his sins out loud because there were no masks worth keeping. In that kind of a moment, with that kind of a presence, we all experience that kind of repentance.

After not saying a word for a few minutes, I started to apologize for all the people who had sexually abused these men. They forgave me, and them. I then began to lead them in prayers that they had already been praying: "I repent. Take my heart. You're my Lord."

I had no clue what I was doing (I still don't), I just knew that Jesus was present, alive, and repetitive. It was almost as if we were all transported to a chapter inside of Matthew or John; as if the prison had become the well in Samaria, the pool of Bethesda, or the wedding feast where ceremonial water was turned into celebratory wine.

Seriously, I have been to a lot of good church services, I've heard a lot of incredible sermons, and I've been exposed to a lot of life-altering ministries—but that night, the gospel was not a teaching to be discussed or a scene to be remembered, it was good news to the poor, it was healing the brokenhearted, and it was setting the captives free.

And the biggest prisoner was me: I was an inmate to my version of the gospel, my interpretation of the gospel, and my rules for gospel engagement. But that evening I understood that the gospel was *His*. Jesus is King and Lord, and as much as He loves me, He's not serving my kingdom or bowing down to my religious ways. I wanted to draw lines of separation and I wanted to find laws that would deprive the depraved. But the Bible said it a long time ago: "[Jesus] *is the atoning sacrifice for our sins, and not only for ours but also for the sins of the whole world.*"[3]

The whole world includes all the men in the Institución Correccional Guerrero; it also includes you and me. I wrote this book because when Jesus took the stones out of my hands, I discovered the most liberating life available—it was like I was born again, again. The difference was that this time, I was born aware of the good news for others, not just for myself.

If my life was the story of John 8, I was behaving like the religious leaders. If my life was the story of John 8, I never saw myself as the woman caught in the act of adultery. If my life was the story of John 8, I never acted as the Christ who stopped the execution.

In that penitentiary, I discovered the gospel story that truly set me free. Now I hope that in the captivity of these next few chapters, you will experience the same…and that you will choose who you're going to be in the story of John 8.

Notes

1. Anne Lamott, *Bird by Bird: Some Instructions on Writing and Life* (New York: Pantheon, 1994), 22.
2. Richard Rohr, *Falling Upward: A Spirituality for the Two Halves of Life* (San Francisco: Jossey-Bass, 2011), 74.
3. 1 John 2:2 NIV.

2

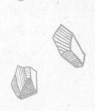

THE TWO CROWDS

"Those who follow Jesus should attract the same people Jesus
attracted and frustrate the same people Jesus frustrated."[1]
—*Shane Claiborne*

Food was the problem: specifically, when Jesus was eating food with *them*…
the tax collectors and sinners. That was the thing that made the Pharisees
and teachers of the Law grind their teeth while they complained with rage.

You can almost feel their disgust when you read the description in
Luke 15:1–2: *"Now the tax collectors and sinners were all drawing near to hear
him. And the Pharisees and the scribes grumbled, saying, 'This man receives
sinners and eats with them.'"*

Yuck!

I'm fascinated with the contrast in these two verses. The crowd that had
gathered around Jesus is clearly defined and delineated. On one side you have
the worst people, and on the other side you have the people who *thought* they
were the best people. They were the less excited part of the crowd—those
who were not there to be near Jesus but rather to find ways to destroy Him.

Notice that the main concern of the religious leaders was not that Jesus
was preaching to the tax collectors and sinners; they did that themselves
and considered it a privilege from Yahweh.

Nor were they complaining about His miracles or His parables; they too could help people on certain days and they too could share stories to educate.

What they hated in this instance was the eating together—the ultimate love language!

When I visit my mom in Puerto Rico, I rediscover this reality. I don't know if it's a brown-people thing or a warm-weather thing, but food is the godliest way to express affection and welcoming.

So much of what Jesus did involved food. His first miracle was turning water into wine and extending a wedding party into legendary status. The way He chose to reveal the mystery of the cross was by offering His body and His blood as the eternal meal. He gathered with His disciples around lunches and brunches and He multiplied the bread and the fish to feed thousands of people on multiple occasions. Jesus invited Himself to people's homes for dinner and He even cooked breakfast for His disciples after the resurrection.

By reading all of this you would think that Jesus was a brown person.... (And here is where I would insert a wink emoticon to express the cute sarcasm of the previous sentence.) #Millennial.

The Son of Man was born and raised in a culture that viewed food as one of the ultimate ways to express companionship and acceptance. The Son of God continually and consistently invited people to His table. However, it was not just the food that was being served, it was the way He looked at the people He was serving. The religious leaders hated the fact that Jesus enjoyed the company of *these* people. *How could He claim to know God and yet be so comfortable with the godless?*

Yuck!

Now, on the other side of the story you have the yucky ones, and Dr. Luke explains to us why they were there: *"The tax collectors and sinners were all **drawing near to hear him**."*

This sacred statement almost becomes an invitation for the church today. As we read it we must ask ourselves, "What are we doing differently from Jesus that makes the tax collectors and sinners of our time not want to be *near us*, and not want to *hear us?*" "What was it about Jesus that made the most immoral people around Him draw to His presence and His teaching?"

Maybe it began with the fact that Jesus did not draw lines between the terms "tax collector" and "sinner." You see, every generation has the one category of sin that deserves its own title. By this time, around AD 27, tax collectors were considered the vilest of people, and I don't blame anyone who judged them. A tax collector was more than just an employee of the Roman IRS; he was also a thief, a traitor, a snitch, and a cheat. They collected more taxes than Caesar required (which made them more evil in the eyes of the Jewish people than the pagan god of Rome). If you chose to be a tax collector you were guaranteed a life of wealth and power but you could also guarantee that your own family would disown you. These lonely guys were so hated by their own people that they had their own category of sinful identification. It was the unstated certainty in all of Judea, "Yes, we are all sinful…but we're not *tax collector* sinful."

More than two thousand years later, we're still doing the same. It varies by nation and generation, but this pattern continues. In some parts the "tax collectors" have been the LGBTQ community, in other areas it is the abortionist/pro-choice crowd, in some circles it's the followers of Mohammed, and in others it's those fundamentalists from the Religious Right.

We categorize each other inside of boxes that feel solid enough to become stepping stones, because we want to use them to boost ourselves higher. Superiority is what we're looking for, and I hate to admit it, but I love the lines that separate us. Sure, I tweet against them, but I am fond of the safety they provide. Finding one sin that is worse than all of my sins makes me feel better about my "minor sin." Finding people who, by my categories, are different (and lesser) makes me feel like I can get ahead.

And this, my friend, is basic human nature.

"I'm bad, but I'm not *that* bad."

"I struggle, *but* I eventually overcome."

"I've missed the mark, *but* not by that far."

The first step toward freedom is admitting to ourselves that *there is* a religious leader raging within us. He is either critical of the work of

Jesus, critical of the people Jesus hangs out with, or critical of the people who don't know Jesus yet. He's in there somewhere and he's robbing us of the opportunity of becoming a true disciple. You see, I have met raging Pharisees in the Religious Right, unbearable Sadducees in the liberal left, and a combination of both of them on the inside of me.

The fact that the culture around Jesus provided a particular category for a specific group of sinner proves that we all struggle with comparison and pride.

That's why, within the context of Luke 15, surrounded by the ones who wanted to hear Him and the ones who hated to see Him, Jesus spoke three of the most beautiful parables ever shared.

And they are required reading for the sinner and the religious leader.

Notes
1. Shane Claiborne, Twitter post, December 18, 2015, 5:43 a.m., http://twitter.com/ShaneClaiborne.

3

THREE PARABLES

"God isn't *fair*: if he were fair, we'd all be in the soup. God is *good*:
crazy, stark-staring-bonkers good."[1]
—*Robert Farrar Capon*

All three of the parables in Luke 15 prove the most radical part of the
New Testament manifesto: *It is God who comes to us*. It is the shepherd that
pursues the sheep. It is the woman who finds the coin. It is the father who
runs toward the son (to hug him and kiss him and throw him a *par-tay*)

This is the heroic counter-argument against religion itself: God loves
us, God finds us, and God becomes us. Tertullian said that *the first reaction to truth is hatred*, and I remember being a Christian and hating the
good news of Christ. I know that sounds insane, but I have met enough
Christians in the last fifteen years to prove this to be true.

Not just true, but prevalent.

Most of Western Christianity loves the name of Jesus (because He
can save "me") but hates the ways of Jesus (because He also wants to save
"them").

There's a radical missionary in Mozambique named Heidi Baker. She
has planted thousands of churches, has fed thousands of orphans, and has

held thousands of people who only knew rejection. I'll let her say it, because her life and surrender prove that theories are cheap but action is sacred:

> [Jesus] loved people back to life. He would go anywhere, talk to anyone. And wherever He went, He would stop for the one—the forgotten one, the one who was rejected, outcast, sick, even stone dead. Even a thief who was dying for his crimes on the cross next to Him. In the Kingdom of God's love there is no sinner who cannot come home.[2]

This is precisely the point of the three parables that Jesus shared with the two crowds in Luke 15. They prove that there is a Savior who is willing to carry sheep, sweep the house, and return the inheritance. And we need this for ourselves!

This book will be anathema unless you know yourself (for yourself) that God loves you this way. The genius of Jesus was to utilize the contrast in the audience in order to transform the perception of God in all people. Both the religious leaders and the sinners in attendance would have been dumbfounded by this fresh and radical perspective—and it seems like the church is still dumbfounded by it. We are still struggling to believe that the God of the universe, who is so holy, big, and mysterious, could also be this lovely, kind, and available. We want to be less judgmental, but we have so many Bible verses that arm us to be judgmental. We want to be less religious but there seems to be so many things to be religious about. We don't want to be the Pharisees or Sadducees but it seems like that is precisely what the world expects from us right now (and we keep falling in the trap).

Christ came to save us from our sin, but He also came to save us from the idea that we could be saviors (or judges) of ourselves, or of anyone else.

This is why we have stop and look to Jesus again (and again, and again). We look to Him because we claim Him to be our Savior, our Beloved, and our King—and there is no other way forward but to do it as He did it. The solution is as simple as the title suggests: *Drop the Stones*. For when we do, we will have free hands to pick up sheep, find coins, and embrace prodigals.

And we must do this, while eating together.

Now let me finish with a *huge* disclaimer: if we never do it, if we hold on to the stones and reject the good news of Jesus for all…He will still feed us, make room for us at His table, and love us…*perfectly.*

Bon Appetite.

Notes

1. Robert Farrar Capon, *The Mystery of Christ: …and Why We Don't Get It* (Grand Rapids, MI: Wm. B. Ecrdmans Publishing Co., 1993), 91.
2. Heidi Baker and Rolland Baker, *Reckless Devotion: 365 Days into the Heart of Radical Love* (Bloomington, MN: Chosen Books, 2014), 47.

4

TRAFFIC LIGHT

"Every time we use religion to draw a line that keeps people out,
Jesus is with the people on the other side of that line."
—*attributed to Rev. Hugh L. Hollowell*

Robert was always hanging out at the traffic light, and he always smelled like death. He used to have a job, a family, and access to a shower, but now he had nothing—no home, no bank account, and no dignity. An addiction to alcohol owned Robert, and, like a slave-master, it drove him to that traffic light. His daily plan was to "earn" a living by begging on the streets of Camuy, Puerto Rico, to see if enough people in this tiny town felt the pity he never felt when he had been the one braking at traffic lights beside the homeless asking for change.

At night, with his nickels and dimes, Robert would buy the liquid that would help him forget. Forty-proof was almost strong enough to erase the reality of his tragic life on the streets.

That specific traffic light was less than two minutes from our church. It was the exact turn that would indicate proximity to the house of God, yet to that house Robert never came.

Almost every day we would encounter each other, and almost every day I prayed that the light would stay in my favor (so that I could drive on by). The days when God would not answer my prayer, I would give Robert all ninety seconds of my attention before the red turned green.

Some days I would get slightly angry with Robert. I would never tell him that of course, but I expected him to do something about his condition. I would whisper to myself, "He should know better; he should try harder; it's up to him what happens next. Yes, God, You love him, but he needs to love himself!"

Then I would smile, roll my window down, throw a few quarters into his plastic cup while saying *"Bless you,"* and then drive to church to do the *will of God.*

After months of people inviting Robert to join them for the Sunday service, one couple was successful. A young man and his wife would take Robert to a restaurant for a weekly meal. Eventually, they took a more personal step: they brought him to their home for rice and beans. They did not stop there. Soon they started to buy him groceries and take him to see the doctor. This couple purposefully did not invite him to church; instead, they became the church to him.

In due course, Robert joined them for their Sunday routine at church. It was close to his spot on the street anyway, and the air-conditioning provided a welcomed break from the heat and the shame.

The first time Robert entered the church I noticed him right away. I could see him from afar and, honestly, it was impossible not to recognize him. I wanted to be kind and prove that I was a cool pastor and a loving Christian, so I made my way over to him. Before I got close, the odor that radiated off of him was more than I could handle. I gave him a short handshake, but as soon as we were done, with half a smile on my face (and trying my best to be discreet), I began a desperate search for hand sanitizer (because who knew where those hands had been).

Robert kept visiting our building and he started to engage in the "full church experience." He would greet people, close his eyes during worship, and even respond to the preacher's invitation. He prayed the Sinner's Prayer on multiple occasions. Per our theology, salvation for his soul seemed guaranteed, but Robert was still lost on the streets, unsaved from himself.

After months of having Robert among us, he began to behave like a proper, proper church member, and in our church that meant moving to the front during ministry time and waiting to be touched by God. There he was, smelly, broken, and yet expectant. And it was in that place that Robert encountered true love.

You see, there was a British girl who would sit next to me (and she always smells amazing). She could barely understand the songs or the sermons because she was still learning Spanish, so she would ask me to translate for her, and even though it was my duty as her husband to make it easy for her to come to church with me, I would quickly get tired of repeating the words and ask her just to pray.

And pray she did.

It was on one of those days, while talking to Jesus, she felt a compulsion to go to Robert and give him a hug. Slowly but confidently she approached him. Wanting to be obedient to God, without making the man feel uncomfortable, she asked Robert in her broken Español, *"Can I give you a hug?"*

The six-foot-six homeless man nodded yes, probably thinking it was another one of the courteous three-second hugs these Christians kept giving him while holding their breath.

Catherine smiled, raised herself like a graceful ballerina, and wrapped her arms around Robert's dirty neck. My wife then held on to him for more than twenty minutes. She squeezed him as if she was hugging me, or her dad, or Jesus Himself. Her calf muscles worked hard as she determined to stay in that position, tiptoeing for the hug. It was like she was convinced that this one act would make up for every unkind word Robert had ever heard—as if one embrace could convince Robert to stop drinking, sinning, begging, limping. She held on to this man like it was her favorite thing to do. And as she breathed in his stench, all she could smell was the fragrance of the Redeemer. While she embraced his wounded body, she could feel herself being healed. And watching her doing it with such grace convicted me.

Catherine was Christ, Robert was the adulterer, and I was the religious leader. *When will I ever learn?*

Previously I had tried my best to convince Robert to change his life-style; I spoke to him on multiple occasions about improving his condition. I invested time in prayer asking God to lead him into the way of real freedom. My strategy was to use godly principles, human plans, and the pious language I was acquainted with, but he still looked the same, begged the same, and drank the same.

It wasn't until that warm embrace that things turned.

We never saw Robert again. We didn't see him on the street or in the church.

Why? Because he decided to go back to his family. Then he entered a rehabilitation program.

Robert moved on to a different sort of light, a more divine and gracious one.

He sent us a message a few months later. He was clean, happy, and connected. "It was the hug," he kept saying. "It was Catherine's hug."

In the captivity of my wife's arms, a drunkard became intoxicated with acceptance. There, he encountered the fragrance of liberty; there, my wife enjoyed the aroma of obedience; and there, I stumbled into the stench of my pride.

Mother Theresa once said, "If you can't do great things, just do little acts of love." I think she knew a thing or two about Jesus. So does my wife. And one day, I hope to smell like them both.

As the Bible says, *"We are the aroma of Christ to God among those who are being saved and among those who are perishing."*[1]

Yes, *"among those who are perishing."*

Notes
1. 2 Corinthians 2:15.

5

THE KNOWLEDGE OF GOOD AND EVIL

*"By judging others we blind ourselves to our own evil and to the
grace which others are just as entitled to as we are."*[1]
—Dietrich Bonhoeffer

Our ability to discern good from evil doesn't actually make us God; it just makes us think we're Him. The serpent in the garden deceived Adam and Eve by making them believe that by eating of the Tree of Knowledge they were going to be like the Almighty, which was actually his own goal. The tragedy is that when they bit the fruit, they looked at themselves and discerned their bodies to be evil. Then they looked at each other and they saw each other as evil. And worst of all, they looked at God, became afraid, and discerned the Father of Lights to be evil.

Bummer.

They *did* receive the ability to discern good from evil, but because it was not meant for them to receive it, they discerned good from evil incorrectly.

The law of Moses is God's answer to the requests of mankind to know right from wrong. The cross of Jesus is our opportunity to transcend the tree in the garden. We are now invited to eat His body and drink His blood and get something that is far superior to Eden—and that table is open to all.

Yet somehow we're still trying to be God ourselves instead of feasting on Him. We're still eating of that first tree, pretending that we're experts in good and evil. We've given ourselves PhDs on right and wrong while failing miserably at life and love. We're like wine snobs who pretend to know a fine Bordeaux from a cheap cabernet, while choking on the taste of sour vinegar mixed with dung. And while ingesting the fruit from the wrong tree, we are becoming what we eat.

When we hear a person speak differently, we point, we judge, and we say, "Evil!" When we work for a boss who is better than the last one, we point, we judge, and we say, "Good!" When we see a person's style of dress, we point, we judge, and we say, "Evil!" When we notice a preacher who sounds like us, we point, we judge, and we say, "Good!"

And the only one with legal standing to judge the nations, says to us,

Judge not, that you be not judged. For with the judgment you pronounce you will be judged, and with the measure you use it will be measured to you. Why do you see the speck that is in your brother's eye, but do not notice the log that is in your own eye? Or how can you say to your brother, "Let me take the speck out of your eye," when there is the log in your own eye? You hypocrite, first take the log out of your own eye, and then you will see clearly to take the speck out of your brother's eye.[2]

We're allowed to help pluck the speck from our brother's eye, but *only* when we are completely free of our log. We must ask ourselves sincerely, *Are we there yet?*

Let's use divorce and homosexuality as a contrasting example.

Apart from the clearly defined rules in the Catholic Church, most of Christianity has not made a fuss about divorce. Notice that Jesus never spoke out against homosexuality directly, but He did speak twice against divorce.[3]

Now, I know that if I reduce this conversation to only that previous statement, it would be inconclusive and irresponsible. There are many Bible verses that discuss different kinds of sexual behaviors, sins, and preferences, and those are all valid and important to discuss (and the church has done a great job of repeatedly letting everyone know about them). But I do want to ask a simple question: why is the church not as outspoken against divorce as it is against homosexuality? If we believe both to be sin, why is one sin treated as a *threat* and the other treated as *part of life?* We can't proclaim the purity of marriage while accepting (and in some cases empowering) the breaking of marriage. We have pastors and leaders, apostles and celebrity preachers who are on their second or third spouse. We download their podcasts, we honor their calling, and we rarely speak of their failures. And facing this, we must remember that Jesus challenged the Pharisees not because they followed the law, but because they twisted the law to only benefit themselves.

Please don't assume that I am anti-divorce; I am pro-hope. I was the first-born in the second marriage for both of my parents. I have two sisters from my dad's first marriage, one sister from my mom's first marriage, and two other sisters from their current union. We are one family. We were raised to love each other and accept the complexity of our tribe. I love and respect both my dad's first wife and my mom's first husband…and I would never call any of my sisters *half*.

But biblically speaking my parents failed to follow the law of God (and the direct invitation from Jesus). Yet, I was born because of their failure. I get to write this book because they were allowed to separate and begin again. I still don't think that divorce is the best case scenario, but God is an expert at turning crap into fertilizer.

Imagine now how it looks to unbelievers when we judge, criticize, and hate those who think about marriage differently than we do, while demonstrating that we think about marriage differently than God does. Just because we are using Bible verses to judge people does not automatically mean that we are judging them biblically. While we use one part of the Bible to condemn *them*, the Bible stares back at us, surprised (perhaps raising an eyebrow), and condemns *us*.

And on and on we go, failing to keep the main thing, the main thing.

I can imagine that if the magnitude of everyone's sin was paraded in public, we would all be a lot more gracious to each other. Plus, Jesus already said it: "If we judge we will be judged."[4] Plain and simple. And this is me not even getting into how much porn pastors view on Sunday, after preaching.[5] How women in the church are more likely to suffer sexual and physical abuse than women outside the church.[6] How children are molested at a higher rate in Christian congregations than in public schools.[7] Yes, the ironic thing about legalism is that it doesn't make people work harder; it makes them give up.

Now God still opposes the proud and gives grace to the humble.[8] And He does it because He loves the prideful too much to let them get away with thinking that they are something that they're not. If we insist on eating of the Tree of the Knowledge of Good and Evil, we will remain deceived, thinking we can truly discern who is good and who is evil. That responsibility belongs only to God. Our responsibility is to tend the garden and deny the serpent's alluring appeal, because to all (divorcées, lesbians, masturbators, and liars) Jesus is the tree of life—and the hour has come for all to taste and see that He is good.

If our major is in Truth but our minor is in Love, we'll keep sounding out of tune. Yes, there is godly space for judgment, but we will talk about that later, once we've fully died to our desire for it. Remember what Paul said in Galatians 6:1–3:

> *"If anyone is caught in any transgression, you who are spiritual should restore him in a spirit of gentleness.* **Keep watch on yourself, lest you too be tempted.** *Bear one another's burdens, and so fulfill the law of Christ. For if anyone thinks he is something, when he is nothing, he deceives himself."*

Ouch.

And amen.

Notes

1. Dietrich Bonhoeffer, *The Cost of Discipleship* (London: SCM Press, 1986), 185.
2. Matthew 7:1–5.
3. See Matthew 19:3–12; Mark 10:2–12.
4. See Matthew 7:2.
5. "Pastors and Porn: The Struggle is Real," CBN News, January 29, 2016, http://www1. cbn.com/cbnnews/us/2016/January/Pastors-and-Porn-The-Struggle-is-Real. (Accessed April 6, 2017).
6. Charlene Aaron, "Domestic Abuse in the Church a 'Silent Epidemic,'" CBN News, February 5, 2016, http://www1.cbn.com/cbnnews/us/2016/January/Combating-Domestic-Abuse-in-the-Church. (Accessed April 6, 2017.)
7. Boz Tchividjian, "Startling Statistics: Child sexual abuse and what the church can begin doing about it," Religion News Service, January 9, 2014, http://religionnews. com/2014/01/09/startling-statistics/. (Accessed April 6, 2017.)
8. See James 4:6.

6

GOD'S ENEMIES

"You can't possibly trust God if you're too busy playing God."
—*Jonathan Martin*

Let me tell you a little bit more about some of the main adversaries of the ministry of Jesus: the Pharisees, the Sadducees, and the Teachers of the Law. Their hatred toward Jesus was primarily due to the fact that He was not presenting the kingdom they wanted, and neither was He asking for the "righteousness" that they were already living.

Now, if we become aware of the specific impulses that Jesus was addressing in the religious leaders then we can address these impulses in ourselves. The main temptation, though, will be to read this short explanation and think of everyone else who acts, behaves, speaks, preaches, and Facebooks like a religious leader. But that would be precisely what a Pharisee/Sadducee/Teacher of the Law would do.

I've heard people use the story of Jesus flipping the tables as validation for their destructive (religious) ways. They even quote Matthew 23 (which we will address soon) as biblical foundation for pointing the finger at those they condemn as "religious leaders." But my question to them (and myself) is this: *Are we also willing to die on the cross for the people we correct? Are we healing them? Washing their feet? Are we serving them as Jesus serves the church?*

If our answer is "no" to any of the above, then we have lost the right to flip any tables. So here they are:

1. **Pharisees:** Their name means "set apart." And their main distinctive was a belief in the oral Law that God gave to Moses along with the Torah, or written Law. For the Jewish people, the Torah is similar to a nation's constitution in the sense that it sets down a series of laws that are open to clarification and interpretation. Pharisees believed that God also gave Moses the knowledge of what these laws meant and how they should be applied. And even more than that, these "set apart" men believed that they were the only ones capable of understanding and sharing the Law. Imagine their frustration when the carpenter's son interpreted the law differently than they did. During the time of Jesus, most people listened to the Pharisees. They were the spiritual authority that the common Jewish family respected. This is why the Word of God Himself began so many of His famous declarations with "you've heard it said...." That way, He could directly counteract things that the Pharisees were incorrectly saying.

2. **Sadducees:** These elitist men rejected the idea of the oral Law and insisted on an exact interpretation of the written Law. Surprisingly though, they were also willing to incorporate Hellenism (Greek culture) into Jewish lifestyle, something the Pharisees hated and opposed. The Sadducees rejected every authority except for the written Scriptures (primarily the Pentateuch) and had their own Book of Decrees, which specified a system of capital punishment: who was to be stoned, who strangled, who burned, and who beheaded (how sweet).

3. **Teachers of the Law:** They were the lay teachers of the Law and they eventually supplanted the priests in the synagogues. In the New Testament, these men were primarily called "scribes," but they are also referred to as "lawyers" and "teachers of the Law." If the Pharisees were the theologians and the Sadducees were the wealthy board members, the Teachers of the Law were more like the local church pastors.

Although Pharisees and Teachers of the Law were frequently the adversaries of Jesus, it was not all bad. Pharisees asked Him to eat with them on a few occasions,[1] and He was also warned of coming danger by some of them. [2] Additionally, it appears that there were Pharisees (including Nicodemus) who believed in Him, although they did so in secret because of the hostility of their leaders toward Yeshua, Hebrew for "Jesus."

Paul himself affirmed his affiliation with the Pharisees in several places. The apostle stated that he was a Jew brought up in Jerusalem at the feet of Gamaliel, a leading Pharisee who helped Peter and the apostles soon after the beginning of the church.[3]

The New Testament shows that Christ did not clash with the Sadducees until near the end of His ministry, mainly because they were more of a political party and not the religious teachers of the people. The Sadducees were less concerned with religion and more concerned with the power they could acquire through the high priesthood and the political system. The Pharisees and Sadducees were the two religious/political "parties" that served in the Great Sanhedrin, a kind of Jewish Supreme Court made up of seventy-one members, whose responsibility was to interpret all civil and religious laws.

Karl Barth thought of "the revelation of God as the abolition of religion."[4]

Can we try this with everyone?

Because the easiest thing in the world would be to point the finger, accuse the religious, and stay away from their systems. Nonetheless, Jesus engaged not just the tax collectors and sinners but also the religious leaders of His time. They criticized Him, mocked His teachings, and took part in the plot to kill Him. But we need to always remember that Jesus died for the hypocrisy of the men who accused the condemned woman as much as He died for the woman herself. We have to identify the self-righteousness in ourselves so we can surrender it again, knowing beyond a shadow of a doubt that Christ loves us, believes in us, and will endure with us till the end.

Oh yes, we will speak the truth of Christ in the face of the horrible man-made systems that continue to corrupt the message of grace. But we do so in full awareness that *"our struggle is not against flesh and blood, but against the rulers, against the authorities, against the powers of this dark world."*[5]

Notes

1. See Luke 7:36; 11:37; 14:1.
2. See Luke 13:31.
3. See Acts 5:33–39.
4. Karl Barth, *Church Dogmatics*, Vol. 1, Pt. 2 (Edinburgh: T. & T. Clark, 1956), 280.
5. Ephesians 6:12 NIV.

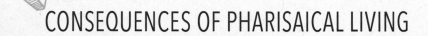

7

CONSEQUENCES OF PHARISAICAL LIVING

Hola amigo,

Thank you for making it to chapter 7. This letter is an effort to explain what is about to happen, because what I'm sharing next is quite possibly the nastiest part of the New Testament. I fought with my editors about this, because as a rule you never put such a long extract of Scripture in the middle of your writing (and especially not this extract).

"It's better to comment about it and simply reference the Bible citation in the footnotes," they said.

"Most people will skip it," they said.

"You will lose the readers' interest," they said.

The experts might be right. But how could I skip such a powerful, moving, and disturbing sermon?

Maybe if I explain to you why I'm doing it, it will help you to better digest it.

Maybe.

Here is Jesus speaking to the people about the religious authority of His time. These leaders have been nagging him with questions, challenges, and unbelief; so Jesus responds with one of His longest, most uninterrupted speeches.

If I stood up in most modern churches, without telling them that Jesus said this Himself, and just preached (word by word) the verses that you're about to read, I would probably never be invited again (and I love being invited again).

Now, because I love you, I have chosen to give you *The Message* version to make it as accessible as possible to our context and our conversation. #ThankYouEugene.

And you've got to trust me, 95 percent of everything I preach, teach, and write about is on the love of God. But seeing as this is Jesus speaking, and Jesus is the image of God, and God is pure unfiltered love, I will leave this here and exit quietly.

See you on the other side.

Hugs,

Carlos

Matthew 23:1-34

Jesus turned to address his disciples, along with the crowd that had gathered with them. "The religion scholars and Pharisees are competent teachers in God's Law. You won't go wrong in following their teachings on Moses. But be careful about following them. They talk a good line, but they don't live it. They don't take it into their hearts and live it out in their behavior. It's all spit-and-polish veneer.

"Instead of giving you God's Law as food and drink by which you can banquet on God, they package it in bundles of rules, loading you down like pack animals. They seem to take pleasure in watching you stagger under these loads, and wouldn't think of lifting a finger to help. Their lives are perpetual fashion shows, embroidered prayer shawls one day and flowery prayers the next. They love to sit at the head table at church dinners, basking in the most prominent positions, preening in the radiance of public flattery, receiving honorary degrees, and getting called 'Doctor' and 'Reverend.'

"Don't let people do that to you, put you on a pedestal like that. You all have a single Teacher, and you are all classmates. Don't set people up as experts over your life, letting them tell you what to do. Save that authority for God; let him tell you what to do. No one else should carry the title of 'Father'; you have only one Father, and he's in heaven. And don't let people maneuver you into taking charge of them. There is only one Life-Leader for you and them—Christ.

"Do you want to stand out? Then step down. Be a servant. If you puff yourself up, you'll get the wind knocked out of you. But if you're content to simply be yourself, your life will count for plenty.

"I've had it with you! You're hopeless, you religion scholars, you Pharisees! Frauds! Your lives are roadblocks to God's kingdom. You refuse to enter, and won't let anyone else in either.

"You're hopeless, you religion scholars and Pharisees! Frauds! You go halfway around the world to make a convert, but once you get him you make him into a replica of yourselves, double-damned.

"You're hopeless! What arrogant stupidity! You say, 'If someone makes a promise with his fingers crossed, that's nothing; but if he swears with his hand on the Bible, that's serious.' What ignorance! Does the leather on the Bible carry more weight than the skin on your hands? And what about this piece of trivia: 'If you shake hands on a promise, that's nothing; but if you raise your hand that God is your witness, that's serious'? What ridiculous hairsplitting! What difference does it make whether you shake hands or raise hands? A promise is a promise. What difference does it make if you make your promise inside or outside a house of worship? A promise is a promise. God is present, watching and holding you to account regardless.

"You're hopeless, you religion scholars and Pharisees! Frauds! You keep meticulous account books, tithing on every nickel and dime you get, but on the meat of God's Law, things like fairness and compassion and commitment—the absolute basics!—you carelessly take it or leave it. Careful bookkeeping is commendable, but the basics are required. Do you have any idea how silly you look, writing a life story that's wrong from start to finish, nitpicking over commas and semicolons?

"You're hopeless, you religion scholars and Pharisees! Frauds! You burnish the surface of your cups and bowls so they sparkle in the sun, while the insides are maggoty with your greed and gluttony. Stupid Pharisee! Scour the insides, and then the gleaming surface will mean something.

"You're hopeless, you religion scholars and Pharisees! Frauds! You're like manicured grave plots, grass clipped and the flowers bright, but six feet down it's all rotting bones and worm-eaten flesh. People look at you and think you're saints, but beneath the skin you're total frauds.

"You're hopeless, you religion scholars and Pharisees! Frauds! You build granite tombs for your prophets and marble monuments for your saints. And you say that if you had lived in the days of your ancestors, no blood would have been on your hands. You protest too much! You're cut from the same cloth as those murderers, and daily add to the death count.

"Snakes! Reptilian sneaks! Do you think you can worm your way out of this? Never have to pay the piper? It's on account of people like you that I send prophets and wise guides and scholars generation after generation—and generation after generation you treat them like dirt, greeting them with lynch mobs, hounding them with abuse."

Hi again.

Welcome back. I'm glad you made it.

Now let me show you how people can fall into this kind of deception.

Here is my legitimate warning of The Consequences of Pharisaical Living.

Starring me.

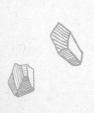

8

CARLOS A. RODRÍGUEZ,
FRAUD EXTRAORDINAIRE

"God will never anoint the fake you, so stop pretending."
—*attributed to Heather Jackson*

As a young preacher, pastoring a growing local church, 2014 could have not started better. I had multiple invitations to preach in different nations, and in my line of work, that is feasting atop the food chain.

In January, my wife and I were on stage on the first day of a superb conference in Toronto. We were leading the meeting, looking picture-perfect, and getting more and more recognition in our charismatic-Christian world.

By April, I was releasing my first book and traveling back to Canada to be the keynote speaker at a major youth conference. Then I was off to Romania, England, Peru, and Colombia, with other trips and invitations around the USA. I was preaching mostly to big crowds, selling tons of books, and getting lucrative offerings.

So yeah, I was killing it.

Yet the more I became an expert at God, the less I seemed to know Him. Somehow, I stopped doing the elementary parts of our faith: talking to Jesus, dying to ambition, being kind with my words, and serving the least. Worst of all, I became violent at home; punching holes through the wall, cursing at my wife, getting rough physically, and being a total jerk to her in front of the kids.

The bigger my platform, the bigger my blind spot became. So I didn't notice that my spouse was super unhappy, that my heart was tired and bitter, that my kids were desperate for my attention, and that my friends were more distant than ever.

I was so blinded by my ego that I became angrier and more depressed.

And of course…everyone else was to blame.

"The devil is attacking me!"

"My childhood was so difficult!"

"Church is too demanding!"

"Catherine is so selfish!"

And on and on I believed and sinned.

When we are struggling with ugly behavior and patterns of iniquity, the only way forward is to take responsibility for our part and let God be responsible for everything else. And it's somewhat compulsory to discover the painful truth that *who you are when no one is looking, is who you really are.*

Who was I when no one was looking? A stone-throwing, abusive husband, who dishonored the people he worked with and pretended to be holy and connected to heaven.

After a stagnant time of not seeing progress on my part, my courageous wife fortunately spoke up. She asked for help; she demanded I make needed changes, but to my eyes, my calling was hanging on the words of the woman who was ratting me out to my leaders. I hated her for it, because from my screwed-up perspective, she was kiboshing my success. It took me months to realize that there was actual deep sin and transgression.

After years of teaching about God's incredible identity and sonship, I would never imagine that the most liberating thing He would ever say to me was, *"Carlos, you're the problem."*

My pastors said the same.

As did the counselor.

And my friends.

And God again.

So yeah, I was the problem.

The horrific process began. I lost my position as the lead pastor of the church. I lost my invitations to preach and travel and make more sales. I lost the respect of leaders, pastors, and family members. I was forced into marriage counseling, lots of personal ministry, two retreats in the mountains (for more ministry and counseling), and a couple of months of feeling like the scum of the earth. I was convinced that everyone was out to get me. I looked at my behavior and thought that everyone was overreacting. I drowned in my excuses: "I've been so good," "A lot of people struggle with anger," "Compared to other husbands, I'm a saint!" and on and on.

I even made a contrast of my "fall from grace" with that of other preachers and thought that I was doing amazing and that they sucked in their recovery.

"Ok, ok, I need to work on a few things…but we all do…right?"

At the root of it all, the main problem was that I kept telling everyone, "My family was the priority," but I lived like full-time ministry was the priority. I would feel so proud about the fact that I had never been unfaithful to my wife with another woman while completely missing the fact that I was being unfaithful to her with the bride of Christ.

My arrogance blindsided me to the point that I did not even realize how destructive my behavior was. The ability to deliver a sermon, to make an invitation, and to entertain the masses had become the ultimate definer of my identity. The title of "pastor" had become "my precious." The opportunities to preach became my confirmation. And the gospel of Jesus was the tool to build my own kingdom.

To quote Richard Rohr one last time, "The ego hates losing, even to God."[1]

Oh, yes, it does.

With all of my heart I hated that season of walking in the light. I was a full-blown Pharisee—scary, furious, deceived. Or in the words of Jesus (who loves me so well):

You're hopeless, you religion scholar and Pharisee! Fraud! You're like a manicured grave plots, grass clipped and the flowers bright, but six feet down it's all rotting bones and worm-eaten flesh. People look at you and think you're [a saint], but beneath the skin you're [a] total [fraud].[2]

Through the fall of 2014 (pun intended), I mostly stayed home, quiet, bitter and thoughtful. Watching reruns of *Breaking Bad* while "breaking bad" myself. The "expert in God" becoming an expert in pain. Yet immersed in that pain, I reencountered the God I'd been teaching the world about.

One evening I was crying hard, repenting to my wife, and asking her to forgive my outbursts and gross dishonor again. And there I had the strangest/strongest sense of Jesus saying to me, "I'm proud of you." That would have been a perfect moment for God to correct me, challenge me, or speak more discipline. (He has done all three in the past, and as a father myself, I understand how they are necessary.) But in the lowest point of life, God reminded me about the heights of His love. His kindness led me to repentance. You know, the kind of repentance where you actually change your direction, you stop blaming others, and you begin to properly heal.

Yes, that (beautiful) kind.

Slowly but surely, I began to realize that Catherine is my ultimate calling. Then, I began to understand that my boys are my main disciples and that my family is the most important congregation.

I also began to respect my audience sincerely (including at church, in print, and on social media) and began to feel comfortable with my weaknesses and theirs.

Now the plan is to continue the transformation, to keep growing in the midst of change, and to allow God to father me into everything He has for me. And even though my titles have changed, the opportunities have changed, and my priorities have changed, God's love will always be the same.

For all of us.

Sometimes it feels appropriate to throw stones at ourselves. Or at least, to allow others to throw rocks freely. We have been sinful, destructive, and bad, so we feel condemned and guilty, worthy of the shame. Yet it is in those very moments when the Son of God bends down to the ground and begins to write in the dirt.

We want to punish ourselves, but the Spirit wants to comfort us. We want to declare ourselves guilty, but the righteous Judge wants to deliver us. We want to discredit ourselves, but Abba calls us *His righteousness*.

And if you're aware of your sin in this moment, I invite you to be more aware of His transcendent grace. May there be hope alive in you again.

Today, I love my family more and more, and my wife and I are connecting like never before. We went from talking divorce to almost finishing the adoption of our baby girl. We have rekindled not just our love, but also our friendship, and I am grateful for her courage, her kindness, and her company.

My two gorgeous boys are getting more hilarious and more delicious every day. I get to really focus on being their dad and there is no greater joy than to pastor them through wrestling, playing Minecraft, and walks in the woods.

I'm also preaching again, serving at the local church, writing books, and walking with a limp. Most of all, I'm staying close to the One who's always been faithful to me.

Three years ago, I hit rock bottom.

I went from full-time ministry to full-time misery.

But my family (both in England and Puerto Rico) loved me through it. My leaders were patient during the restoration. And God was constant even when I wasn't.

Can I encourage you to radically accept whatever you're struggling with? You don't have to embrace it as part of your identity, but the more you humble yourself and recognize your need for help, the closer you will be to your breakthrough.

This is why Jesus spoke Matthew 23. He was not shaming the religious leaders, he was saving them from themselves. Tough love is a real (godly) thing folks. The problem is that we like to focus on the *tough* while Jesus likes to focus on the *love*.

A lot of us need saving from ourselves. Our patterns of sin and addiction have controlled our private lives. Our desire to be loved by others has made us unlovely to the ones who matter most. Our ambition for significance has blinded us from what is actually significant. And sometimes, the price of restoration and reconciliation is called "swallowing your pride" and "admitting that you're wrong."

This was true for me.

Maybe it's true for you.

You might have reached the point where you need to radically accept your frailty so you can radically embrace the love of God. He will meet you where you are, not where you should be, and when you allow Him to begin the process, it might sound like "My child, this is the problem." There, you listen, you humble yourself, and you make room for healing.

Jesus cares more about our hearts than our ministries. Our character matters more than our anointing. And if we are willing to face our worst, in the light of His best, the Savior is ready to do more saving.

Are you the woman caught in the act of adultery or the religious leaders caught in the act of hypocrisy? Either way, listen to His melody once again. *"Neither do I condemn you; go, and from now sin no more."*[3]

Notes
1. Rohr, *Falling Upward*, 47.
2. Matthew 23:27–28 msg, changed from plural to singular.
3. John 8:11.

9

LOVING THE MESS

"The church is a flawed and human institution,
for whom I always have hope."[1]
—*Stephen Colbert*

No matter how much the church needs to be challenged, my challenge is to keep believing in the church. Not because she's perfect, but because she belongs to Him (and I'm part of her). After my year of death, grave, and resurrection, I began to be aware of many things I had not been aware before. My eyes were open to both the beauty and the hypocrisy of modern church life. My heart was like a sponge that could absorb the healing that the family of God provided as much as the madness it inflicted on others. I was shocked at how bipolar my emotions were every Sunday morning, yet after a season of pain and transformation, I began to love the body of Christ again.

But I was still awake.

It was necessary before my breakdown to sustain the illusion. This was the machine that gave me a platform. Whatever the church did and said I agreed with because it was paying the bills. Now, I see all around me a revolutionary tension in the church that is both prophetic and necessary… but the only way for it to stay prophetic and useful, is the way of love.

That is our distinctive.

Religion, spirituality, and theology tend to be destructive when they're not drenched in humility and honor. And I know this as a fact, Jesus loves His own body. He is very comfortable in His own skin, He is not self-conscious about His physique, and unlike me (after three months of winter-bingeing), He looks in the mirror and honors every part of Himself.

Completely.

You and I are the body of Christ, and somehow He loves every wrinkle, bruise, and flabby bit. Yes, Jesus really loves the church, even when you and I don't.

The Bible says that "*You are the body of Christ and individually members of it.*"[2] That means that together we are His body, but in it, there is still room to be individuals. Paul made this distinction clear; some are eyes, some are legs, some are elbows (and hopefully no one is the appendix).[3]

We all belong, we all have a place, and we are all part of Him! And not just a part, but spiritually and experientially, Christ.

I think the apostle really understood this concept because the very first thing Jesus said to him was, "*Saul, why are you persecuting me?*"[4] Paul, who was Saul before this encounter, must have been confused at the moment, because he had never actually interacted with the man Jesus Christ. He knew of Him, he rejected His teachings and murdered His people, but the actual man Jesus he had never met. However, in the blinding light on the road to Damascus, he heard the divine voice and understood, *if I persecute the church, I persecute the Lord (and vice versa).*

It has been more than fifteen years of full-time church ministry for me. During that time, I have been a youth pastor, a worship pastor, a lead pastor, and a whatever-you-need-me-to-be pastor. I have worked in the media department, drama club, sound booth, welcome team, security, counseling, and casting out demons crew. I have done things I did not like, things I did not agree with, and things I felt manipulated into doing. And I loved most of it. I have cleaned toilets by myself, preached to thousands at a time, traveled to more than thirty nations with the gospel, and hated about 246 church members.

Yet, every one of those brothers and sisters (who felt like ugly distant cousins at the time) became the glorious invitation to walk as my Savior walks.

I can say that there have been moments when I have felt disgusted with the politics, the stupidity, and the falsehood of church, yet every single time (and I mean *every* single time), Jesus has shared His thoughts about His body through this one question, *"Carlos, why are you persecuting Me?"*

When you love God but hate the church, you have to understand that God loves you *and* He loves the church...just as much. I know that there are scenarios in which the church has earned the right to be hated, but Jesus is still the same yesterday, today, and forever.

Now let me warn you, the church might provide a sustainable community for a while, but I guarantee that if you stick around long enough, that community will fail you. Church might also provide enough spiritual activity to satisfy your religious hunger, but I can guarantee that eventually you will get bored and complacent. Church might even provide a sense of growth, change, and improvement, but eventually you will fail again, sin again, hurt again, and I can guarantee, someone in the church will reject you for your failures.

So don't come for the community, the spiritual activity, or the self-improvement, come to carry your cross. Embrace your role in the body and destroy the selfish-proud-self-centered-you. Focus on the Servant, King, and resurrected Jesus Christ...who loves you and me and all those 246.

The Godhead left us this very imperfect model, so that in our collective imperfection, we would encounter His perfect love.

Saying to Jesus, "I hate the church" is like telling my wife that she is fat and ugly. I might be "right" according to my very "wrong" standards of beauty and vanity, but I am obviously and terribly wrong (and dumb) for saying it.

Value in the kingdom has never been about what we see; it's always been about what God says. And He says that we are *"a chosen race, a royal priesthood, a holy nation, a people for his own possession."*[5]

I know you have legitimate reasons to disagree with me. The church has hurt many hearts, it has broken good families, and it has produced way too much cheese. But (and it is a very *big* but) it has been, and still is, His body—together, individually, united, God's family.

Yes! Change must come. Reformation is due. Revival is imperative. And we're not in the business of maintaining false unity and non-transformative peace. We will resist the strongholds that sustain ungodly systems of racism and sexism inside the family of God. We will never be okay with manipulation and control; it is not the way of the kingdom and it will not be our way.

But I want us to be part of the generation that is a natural autoimmune system for the body, and not a generation that acts as the poison of chemotherapy attacking from the outside.

Both want healing.

One is healthy.

"If anyone says, 'I love God,' and hates his brother, he is a liar; for he who does not love his brother whom he has seen cannot love God whom he has not seen." This is 1 John 4:20 and it is required material for our hearts and their judgmental inclinations.

Remember the words of Nicky Gumbel: "What unites the church is infinitely more important than what divides us."[6]

There's no need to box this conversation. It can be big, it can be small, it can be old-school, or it can be hipster-relevant…but choose. Find the ideal part of the body where you can serve. The gathering where you and I can join regularly to say, *Jesus is alive! And despite our differences, that is worth celebrating together.* Who cares if it's ten thousand people in a stadium or just three souls gathering in a home, what matters is that you are there (because Lord knows, the body of Christ needs you there). We need your story and your pain, your talents and your convictions, your tensions and your iron.

I used to preach this kind of message as a pastor because I wanted more people in my seats, so there would be more heads to count, a bigger attendance number. Every week I used to invite others into this revelation because I wanted people to get involved and help build my own little pathetic kingdom, but I am now convicted to preach it (and live it) for the sake of His.

Notes

1. Quoted in Barbie Latza Nadeau, "Stephen Colbert Opens Up About His Devout Christian Faith, Islam, Pope Francis, and More," *The Daily Beast*, September 9, 2005, http://www.thedailybeast.com/articles/2015/09/09/stephen-colbert-opens-up-about-his-devout-christian-faith-islam-pope-francis-and-more.html. (Accessed March 18, 2017.)
2. 1 Corinthians 12:27.
3. See verses 15–26.
4. Acts 9:4.
5. 1 Peter 2:9.
6. Reported by Carey Lodge, "Nicky Grumbel: A divided world demands a untied church," *Christianity Today*, May 5, 2015, https://www.christiantoday.com/article/nicky.gumbel.a.divided.world.demands.a.united.church/53299.htm. (Accessed March 27, 2017.)

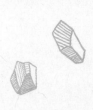

10

FREMDSCHÄMEN

"Church should be so full of laughter and unbridled joy
that outsiders press their noses against our windows
longing to get into the party."[1]
—*Ray Cortese*

You know that terrible feeling when someone is singing out of tune? Like really badly? In front of everybody, and they have no clue how bad it's going? That feeling is called *fremdschämen*, a German term that describes the process of being vicariously embarrassed by someone else. For example, "Tom was completely wasted while he awkwardly slurred his speech at Alex's wedding."

Fremdschämen.

That's how I feel 98 percent of the time I watch Christian TV, or see a Christian Bible verse with a super corny Jesus in the background on Pinterest. I feel this way when I hear a 1990s-sounding Christian song playing on the radio in 2017, watch a Christian movie in the theater that rightly gets an 11 percent rating on Rotten Tomatoes, or, worst of all, when I watch a religious Christian talk politics on the news.

Fremdschämen.

Yes, I hate the critic in me! But I can't deny it: I'm embarrassed by my spiritual family. And so many like me have decided to stay away. They're choosing Netflix over GOD TV, *The Tonight Show* over *The 700 Club*, Jennifer Lawrence in *Catching Fire* over Nicolas Cage and/or Kirk Cameron in any *Left Behind* movie.

Why? Because it is so hard to put ourselves through that misery.

It is a burden that we cannot bear!

Now the problem is that I feel like I am contradicting Scripture. The apostle Paul said in Romans 1:16, *"I am not ashamed of the gospel, because it is the power of God that brings salvation to everyone who believes"* (NIV).

Yet, I feel so ashamed.

I can't help it.

And the worst thing about it is that, as a pastor who has done multiple live events, recorded worship music, and been on Christian television, I am most ashamed of myself!

The good news is that I'm starting to realize that the gospel is different from Christianity. The gospel Paul talks about is God's perfect statement of love and grace. Christianity is the human response to that message. The gospel is the good news of salvation, to all people, everywhere. Christianity is the imperfect expression of the people who have received and acknowledged that news as good. The gospel is the finished work of Christ. Christianity is the unfinished work of men.

I am a Christian—110 percent.

I don't deny our label, but my faith has little to do with Christianity and everything to do with Christ Himself. You see, Jesus was not a Christian. Neither did the first church or the first disciples call themselves Christians. The word *Christian* was not used until Acts 11:26, when it was used against them by others as an insult.

There are multiple stories in the Bible of people who received salvation (and will meet us in paradise) who never once called themselves a "Christian." They never prayed the sinner's prayer, never heard Chris Tomlin or United, never watched *War Room*, and they're doing pretty great.

I know it is human nature to highlight the negative; so I intentionally remember and honor the millions of Christ-followers who are loving their families and being a light in their communities, all over the world. There is an incredible amount of talent and creativity that has been produced by amazing Jesus-followers and the tsunami of that light is growing quickly.

It's also okay for us to admit it when an expression of Christianity does not suit our style, age, or preference. That's the beauty of family! We can honor and celebrate each other without having to be exactly the same.

Yes, I'm a pastor in a superb Christian church (shout out to my Catch the Fire Raleigh-Durham family). I love my Christian friends and coworkers, I'm excited to serve in a global Christian ministry. Nevertheless, I will not settle for the expression of the gospel that we are currently putting out there. Jesus did not die to create a Sunday morning gathering; He gave His life for everyone we encounter Monday through Saturday. Our main message is not to defend Chick-fil-A for closing on Sundays. Our main message is to share God's love with the strip club down the road. Our voice is not mainly for deciding who rules in the White House. Our true power is when we work for the benefit of our cities, our leaders, and our enemies.

Media and politics are a secondary place for the gospel. Our primary platform is with our families, in the gutter with the homeless, with the orphans and the widows, and with the poorest of the poor. That's where the Rock of the Ages invested much of His efforts. And from that place we can *speak truth to power* with authentic authority.

Many are the voices who want to take over the seven mountains of influence. I much prefer to serve them.

Also, I want to keep my heart sweet. I can't be the judge of what is cool, valid, or properly "Christian" (God knows I'm getting old and cheesy myself). *What do I know anyway?*

Our Christian family is a two-thousand-year-old organism that is constantly changing and shifting, and I am honestly excited for the diverse ways that the church is maturing, uniting, and rejecting its own religiosity. Yes, the road is long and tedious, but it would be helpful if analysts like me could invest more time loving and honoring in order to see the unity necessary in the body.

Still, change must come.

That's the perfect tension.

We love the church despite the inconsistencies, but we will not be content with staying inconsistent. The world has to know the true and living Christ: the One who was a Friend of sinners, who was the enemy of religion, who loved people more than events, and who had had enough of the religious/spiritual expression in His own era and came to show us a new (and better) way.

So the next time you feel *fremdschämen* rising up in your heart, smile big. Thank the good Lord for the person/movie/show/preacher who is making you cringe on the inside and get excited for the change you and they will bring to the system. The truth is that they are on TV/stage/radio because they have put in the time and effort to follow what they thought was right. Now, let them become an invitation to you that says, "It's my time!" And let us all use the energy we have been wasting on pointing the finger and turn it into an investment of imagination and sweeping transformation.

It's not a sin to be embarrassed by an expression of Christianity that does not look like Christ. The sin is in judging them, while doing nothing yourself.

As Jesus said when the disciples complained about a "different" member of the family, *"Do not stop him, for the one who is not against you is for you."*[2]

Notes

1. Ray Cortese, Twitter post, February 27, 2015, 4:07 p.m., http://twitter.com/RayCortese.
2. Luke 9:50.

11

THE LOCAL STONE-THROWER

"The beginning of love is to let those we love be perfectly
themselves, and not to twist them to fit our own image." [1]
—*Thomas Merton*

Somehow my heart believed the lie again, "You are right on this one,
Carlos! You definitely understand Jesus. Truth is on your side, you saint-
like Puerto Rican."

And in the belief of such stupidity, I became what I was against: a
stone-thrower.

Yes.

One of those.

A few years back I released a few articles online that were critical of two
Christian leaders and their ministries. I used their names, their images,
and the conveniently selected video clips that pointed out their greed.

In less than forty-eight hours, two of my own leaders approached me.
I was ready to hear their points of view but I wrongly anticipated that they
wanted to control my content. They did exactly the opposite; they loved me
through disagreements, they called me to a higher place, and they invited
me back to the message of grace. I am grateful for their fathering. As Jon

Acuff brilliantly said, "Leaders who can't be questioned end up doing questionable things."

I relearned something in those meetings: people are in need of correction, but that is always done in the context of relationships, because if there is no relationship, then we have not earned the right to correct. That is what my friends did to me, and that is what I should have done to others.

I love to challenge the church with the words of the Head of the church. But that gives me no authority to directly correct other leaders in the body of Christ, unless I know them personally or have served them enough to earn that privilege. (See Matthew 18:12–17 for the appropriate way to do this, according to Jesus.)

I've had to deny the self-imposed jurisdiction to call them out through my platforms. I need the gospel just as much as the people I preach the gospel to. Leaders, sinners, theologians, and weirdos, we need each other and we need the Father's grace. And the reminder from Paul is to *"Be completely humble and gentle; be patient, bearing with one another in love."*[2]

I started blogging because I wanted to tell the broken to have hope, and to tell the church to throw fewer stones. Yet somehow, while trying to do both, I lost hope and I picked up a few rocks. Most of my articles are internal wrestling matches that get nine hundred words of the reader's attention. Nothing I say is the gospel truth (except when I quote Jesus in the gospel truth).

So I ask your forgiveness for the times I nudge you to judge the church as opposed to love it more. I repent for judging styles and denominations, for criticizing leaders in different organizations, and I repent for throwing stones.

To fix the problem of the church being too judgmental toward the world, we cannot become too judgmental toward the church. To address the hypocrisy in church leadership, we can't be hypocritical toward church leaders. The "right" judgments won't fix anything, but trusting God with His people will. This works both ways: *if your theology makes you feel superior to others, rethink your theology.*

And note that approaching influencers with humility (and a willingness to learn from their experiences) actually opens the door for them to be stretched by our innovation and faith. Gathering at the table of Jesus with the Peters and the Gamaliels and the Thomases allows us to be transformed by Christ and each other. The more I walk as family toward the family of God, the more I get to influence my brothers and sisters. And the most productive journey I take in life is in meeting them halfway.

Jesus is always saying, "He who is free of sin, throw the first stone." One generation wants Him to throw stones at sinners; another generation wants Him to throw stones at church leaders. For two thousand years, men have kept trying to get Jesus to throw a stone at the people on the opposite side. Nevertheless, even though He's the only one free from sin, He never will.

So I'll leave you with this quote by Gene Edwards from the masterful book *A Tale of Three Kings*, a book I find myself rereading every other year: "Any young rebel who raises his hand against a Saul, or any old king who raises his hand against an Absalom, may—in truth—be raising his hand against the will of God."[3]

Davids, let's repent our way into the Father's will. Let's forgive the leaders we have judged; let's stop being legalists and critics; and let us move together to the highest standard of grace.

It must start with us.

Notes

1. Thomas Merton, *No Man Is an Island* (Boulder, CO: Shambhala Publications, 2005), 177.
2. Ephesians 4:2.
3. Gene Edwards, *A Tale of Three Kings: A Study in Brokenness* (Carol Stream, IL: Tyndale House Publishers, 1992), 76.

12

LOVELY WEIRDOS

"Only the Bible and we dry up. Only the Spirit
and we blow up. But Word and Spirit, we grow up."[1]
—*John Wimber*

You've probably noticed already that I'm a comfortable *charismatic*. This is one of the appropriate terms used to describe my tribe. And don't worry, I'm not trying to convert you; I just want to give you access to my Christian experience.

We Pentecostal/charismatics are the ones who believe that the manifestations of the Holy Spirit seen in the first-century church—healing, miracles, and speaking in tongues—are available to Christians and can be experienced today.

We make up 8.5 percent of the world's population and 27 percent of all Christians. And our branch of Christianity is second in size only to the Roman Catholic Church.[2] As Sarah Bessey wrote,

> While many strains of the church decline in influence, Pentecostals and charismatics continue to grow by leaps and bounds, particularly in the Global South. The church overall is looking more and more charismatic. Even more traditional denominations recognize charismatic experiences and awakenings worldwide. The Southern

Baptist Convention's International Mission Board recently lifted their ban on members speaking in tongues. And two of the biggest movements in Christianity right now, Hillsong and Bethel, are staunchly, unapologetically, and deeply charismatic/Pentecostal in their language, theology, expression, and passion.[3]

I vividly remember the first time I heard a guy speaking in tongues. It made *such* an impression on me, and this was after listening to the testimony of a man who was healed of HIV, which made an even *bigger* impression on me. Then I saw a few hundred people breaking into song while my mom played the tambourine (to perfection), and that is *still* making an impression on me.

The first time I "fell under the power," I was in a Catholic mass with my high school girlfriend, trying to win over her mom and making fun of the weird priest who was praying for healing and casting out demons.

Oh yeah, we are comfortable with terms like casting out demons, third-heaven experience, and getting drunk in the Spirit.

Kind of comfortable.

And yes, it happened to me first during a Catholic mass.

Trust me, I know how weird we worship and pray and wave our flags. But this is my family, and as self-conscious as I feel sometimes, I will not deny them…us…me…Him…ever.

More than that, I can't deny the results. Every time I have felt God's presence (even when I have struggled to understand it) I have left those experiences more in love with Christ, hungry for His words, and with a renewed willingness to love others.

According to Jesus, "You shall know a tree by its fruit," and the fruit of the charismatic experiences in my own life has been very good.

Of course, like every other branch of Christianity, there is both good and bad. I have personally seen abuse and spiritual manipulation in our charismatic churches. I am still concerned with our eschatology and I have issues with our inconsistent politics and powerful ambitions. I have also seen people with mental issues pretend to be prophets, and men dressed in wedding dresses proclaiming to be the bride of Christ. I have heard unbiblical sermons preached through the veils of spirituality and seen Jesus misrepresented as an angry conservative who hates Muslims. #NotCool.

Yes, charismatic Christianity can be dangerous—it's raw and it's messy. But when I read the Gospels and the book of Acts, I see a few glorious similarities, and I recognize that the worst danger for me would be to completely ignore the Holy Spirit and the family that celebrates His presence.

As Bill Johnson said in his book, *When Heaven Invades Earth*, "If you assign ten new believers the task of studying the Bible to find God's heart for this generation, not one of them would conclude that spiritual gifts are not for today."[4]

There is enough bad about us online (seriously, go check). A lot of it is valid and necessary. Yet, there is also two thousand years' worth of proof that we are credible; still weird, yet still relevant.

Jesus had the Holy Spirit descend on Him like a dove. He performed miracles, signs, and wonders (bizarre ones) and told us that we would do even greater works than Him. Then, in Acts 2, the disciples experienced tongues of fire on their heads, and new tongues in their mouths. Then Paul wrote and affirmed the spiritual gifts in 1 Corinthians 14 and beyond.

And it didn't stop there.

I have cessationist friends (people who believe miraculous spiritual gifts died out with the disciples). Some of my favorite teachers are from mainline churches. I don't believe everyone in the world needs to roll on the floor or shake and quake. But denying the active work of the Holy Spirit (even when it's weird and outdated) would be to deny half of Scripture (and a third of the body of Christ alive today). As the founder of Methodism, John Wesley wrote,

> I was fully convinced of what I had once suspected…that the grand reason why the miraculous gifts were so soon withdrawn was not only that faith and holiness were well-nigh lost, but that dry, formal, orthodox men began even then to ridicule whatever gifts they had not themselves, and to decry them all, as either madness or imposture.[5]

There *is* madness and imposture in the charismatic movement, but there is just as much outside of it. And in the midst of a changing landscape, a new expression of charismatics is arising—a people of love, service, and revival fire. This new prophetic generation is loving the poor, embracing the sacraments, and falling in love with the Jesus of Scripture. They are a bunch of weirdos that are cool with being bizarre, and they are being empowered by the Holy Spirit to change the world.

And I'm proud to be one of them.

Now, let's talk about my extended family.

They got some glorious weirdness going on, as well.

Endnotes

1. John Wimber's Facebook page, https://www.facebook.com/john-wimber-209839175122. (Accessed March 28, 2017.)

2. Pew Forum on Religion and Public Life, *Christian Movements and Denominations*, December 19, 2011, http://www.pewforum.org/2011/12/19/global-christianity-movements-and-denominations/. (Accessed April 10, 2017.)

3. Sarah Bessey, "My Weird Childhood Faith Isn't So Weird Anymore," *Christianity Today*, August, 2015, http://www.christianitytoday.com/women/2015/august/my-weird-childhood-faith-isnt-so-weird-anymore.html. (Accessed March 28, 2017.)

4. Bill Johnson, *When Heaven Invades Earth: A Practical Guide to a Life of Miracles* (Shippensburg, PA: Destiny Image, 1994), 107.

5. John Wesley, *The Works of John Wesley, Volume 3* (Nashville, TN: Abingdon Press, 1986), 60.

13

EXTENSIVE FAMILY

"In necessary things, unity; in doubtful things, liberty;
in all things, charity."[1]
—*Richard Baxter*

The ugly truth is that many Protestants, evangelicals, and charismatics still have nasty things to say about Pope Francis (and the rest of the Catholic Church). The beautiful truth is that things are changing.

Still, go ahead and ask Google, "Is Pope Francis the Antichrist?"

You will get about 380,000 results in 0.32 seconds.

Those stats are from today.

Welcome to Christendom my friends.

You'll find multiple articles, opinions, and suggestions about the Pope being one with Satan himself, an agent from the Illuminati, and a deceitful man who is planning the one-world religion that will destroy us all.

I will say something based on the testimony of people who have met Pope Francis in person. Multiple Christian leaders whom I love and respect (especially my spiritual parents, John and Carol Arnott) have spent time with him and can tell that he loves Jesus like crazy. And with that love, he is changing the world and setting an example for Christ rarely seen in such an influential position.

I know, there are many things I do differently from Pope Francis (and the rest of my Catholic family). I do service, they do mass. I confess on Facebook, they confess in booths. I baptize old, they baptize new. I do jeans, they do robes. But in all the differences of look, style, and tradition, we both preach Christ and Him crucified.

And that's glue enough for God.

For too long Christianity seemed like a religion of powerful white male leaders who were attentive to the wealthy and successful—and we could classify Pope Francis as one of them. Yet, over and over again, we see him in the news, washing the feet of the broken, being playful with children, welcoming refugees into his home, and a doing a lot of the things we all love about our Christian faith.

This generation is attracted to humility. They care about the environment. They stand with the Bible, but they don't want to beat people with it. They are pro-life, but that means every life, from the innocent in the womb to the asylum-seeker in the Middle East to the criminal awaiting execution.

Alas, our message has been hijacked by the political-religious rhetoric of Bible-believing Christians, in contrast with the sound of homosexuals, abortionists, atheists, and liberals (precisely the kind of people Jesus hung out with).

And the Pope's more tolerant attitude resonates with younger Christians.

Ask around, it's hard to find a believer in Christ younger than thirty who does not think the Pope is epic. Of course we're still grateful for the journey the church has taken since the 95 Theses of Martin Luther.

But it's been long enough.

The Protestant Reformation was an important argument within Christendom. It was dangerous, necessary, beautiful, and we honor the bravery of our church fathers in it. However, we are due for a different kind of reformation—one that brings the church together, not one that keeps tearing it apart; one that focuses not on big constructions, denominational agendas, or man-made theologies, but on God's love for people and the good news of salvation. Calling ourselves *Protestants* has become like a prophetic expectation that keeps getting manifested in the horrible comment sections of our blogs and social media posts.

So I'm done with protesting.

I'm a happy charismatic.

I am one in heart with every Catholic, Pentecostal, Lutheran, Methodist, and all others in our family who celebrate the name (and the ways) of Jesus Christ.

Now, according to 1 John 2:22: *"This is the antichrist, he who denies the Father and the Son."* So here are three quotes from the Pope that could help answer the question, Is Pope Francis the Antichrist? (You decide if they sound Anti-Christ or Pro-Jesus.)

1. "I believe in God, not in a Catholic God, there is no Catholic God, there is God and I believe in Jesus Christ, His incarnation."[2]

2. "The Golden Rule also reminds us of our responsibility to protect and defend human life at every stage of its development."[3]

3. "In the roughest moments, remember: God is our Father; God does not abandon His children."[4]

What do you think?

I believe that Jesus is the head of the church; not me, not you, and not Francis. But through us the prayer of Jesus will be answered, *"That they may become perfectly one, so that the world may know that you sent me and loved them even as you loved me."*[5]

I like what author Stacey Campbell said on her Facebook page after meeting with the Pope:

> Had a great meeting with Pope Francis and a small group of evangelical leaders. If we are ever going to be part of answering Jesus' prayer in John 17, we must walk toward, rather than walk away. We were able to discuss key issues on the uniqueness of Christ, the priesthood of all believers, and Pope Francis gave us his book "On Love in the Family." As we approach the 500 year anniversary of the Reformation, we have an opportunity to pray together and speak the truth in love to one another. Truth and love are not mutually exclusive. They go together.[6]

I know the Catholic Church is far from perfect, but every denomination, in one way or another, has been fraudulent and shameful. That's why we need to focus on Christ—because we *all* need the lifeline of redemption.

You know I'm a pastor in a modern charismatic church, and I have no doubts that our unique streams have their place in the great story of redemption.

But we are not enough.

We need our Orthodox family. We need our brothers and sisters in the megachurches. We need the underground church in China as well as our Reformed relatives in America. We need one billion Catholics to join hands together with us in solidarity, in prayer, and in service.

It's true that I met Jesus in the most evangelical event possible (a Billy Graham crusade in 1995), but my life has been thoroughly enriched by not staying exclusively there.

You might have also noticed that I have drawn from almost every stream of Christianity through the different quotes I have shared in this book, because I believe that not one of us owns the full expression of the faith we love. And maybe God made it that way so that we would have to come together.

To learn from each other.

To grow with each other.

And to stop calling each other the *Antichrist*.

Notes

1. Quoted in "Richard Baxter: Moderate in an Age of Extremes," *Christianity Today*, http://www.christianitytoday.com/history/people/pastorsandpreachers/richard-baxter.html. (Accessed March 30, 2017.)
2. Quoted in Eugenio Scalfari, "The Pope: how the Church will change," *Repubblica*, October 1, 2013, http://www.repubblica.it/cultura/2013/10/01/news/pope_s_conversation_with_scalfari_english-67643118/. (Accessed April 3, 2017.)
3. Quoted in Terence P. Jeffrey, "Pope to Congress: Golden Rule Reminds Us of Responsibiltiy to Defend Life at Every Stage of Development," *CNS News*, September 24, 2015, http://www.cnsnews.com/news/article/terence-p-jeffrey/pope-congress-golden-rule-reminds-us-responsibility-defend-life-every. (Accessed April 3, 2017.)
4. Pope Francis, Twitter post, March 10, 2015, 5:00 a.m., http://twitter.com/Pontifex.
5. John 17:23.
6. Stacey Campbell's Facebook page, https://www.facebook.com/Stacey.Campbell.5496, (Accessed March 25, 2017.)

14

DEALING WITH THE JERKS

"The Jesus of the Bible lives by a simple philosophy:
If love guides our hearts, rules become redundant.
Love, embraced as a guiding orientation of other-centeredness,
will always lead us to do the right thing." [1]
—Bruxy Cavey

Allow me to finish Act 1 with a simple step-by-step guide on how to deal with religious people (and for the sake of hyperbole, we'll call them the "religious jerks"). In more than a decade of ministry I have been blessed mightily with hundreds of emails, comments, and love-letters from them. I have read them all, smiled with hope, and drank a few extra glasses of chocolate milk… for comfort.

Religious jerks are usually angry people who justify their hate as spirituality; they dress their bitterness as God's truth and turn their frustration into "holy" manipulation. The problem is not religion, it's actually *self-righteousness*. The New Testament uses the word *religion* in a positive manner, as in, *"religion that God our Father accepts as pure and faultless is this: to look after orphans and widows in their distress and to keep oneself from being polluted by the world."* [2]

Religious jerks are the ones who only live by the second half of that verse. They try hard to keep themselves from being polluted by the world but forget to love and serve the world (by looking after the orphans and the widows).

I've said enough about my religious ways already, so in humility I will try to be lovely, in this Step-by-Step Guide to Dealing with Religious Jerks:

Step 1: Realize that you're a religious jerk yourself.

You might be religious about being non-religious. You might be religious about being gluten-free or lactose-free or anti-_____. We all carry a sense of higher value based on what we do differently from others. It's human nature to compare. So I know that I am a religious jerk myself.

Step 2: The next time there is a natural disaster, be louder with love than the religious jerks are with assumptions.

They might say that God is acting in destructive ways because of the homosexuals, feminists, abortionists, communists, socialists, Obamacare, liberals, pornographers, or whatever. But Jesus is God, and Jesus stopped the storm. Jesus never started one to destroy sinners, He only stopped one to save His friends.

There was also this time when the people in Samaria didn't welcome Jesus. And then, *"When the disciples James and John saw this, they asked, 'Lord, do you want us to call fire down from heaven to destroy them?' But Jesus turned and rebuked them."*[3]

Step 3: (Read above) **Let Jesus rebuke them.**

It's His job, not ours. As Brian Zahnd once tweeted, "Who was Jesus harsh toward? Almost exclusively the scribes and Pharisees. Why? Because they portrayed God as harsh toward sinners."[4]

Let Jesus do it, He can get away with it.

Step 4: Earn it.

Whenever you disagree with a religious jerk, don't become a jerk yourself. Unless you're willing to walk the road of relationship, community, and accountability, engaging in arguments will only bring distrust. The last thing we need is another family feud. Either engage in love-based dialogue or shut it. Remember Proverbs 14:3: *"A fool's mouth lashes out with pride, but the lips of the wise protect them"* (NIV).

Step 5: Don't try to convince them with Bible verses about God's love (they probably know tons of verses about wrath and death and sin).

Instead, talk about the way that the Father has loved you, encouraged you, and been kind to you. Be vulnerable about your weakness and let God show off the strength of His love (and squeeze a few Scriptures in there to make it legit).

Step 6: (I should have started with this one.) **Don't call them religious jerks!** (Not even for hyperbole's sake.)

They are humans, as sinful and as needy as the people they dehumanize, as lovely and as valuable to God as the most innocent child. They each have a name, a story, and incredible value. And for each of them, Jesus bled dry on the cross.

Step 7: Don't judge by appearances.

That's what *most* people hate about religious people. But it's how most people judge a "religious person"—the songs they sing, the clothes they wear, the way they vote, or the things they promote on social media. I have done it hundreds of times, and every time I do, I hear the Holy Spirit lovingly say, *"Who made you better than them?"* Or as James wrote in his formidable letter,

> *Do not slander one another. Anyone who speaks against a brother or sister or judges them speaks against the law and judges it. When you judge the law, you are not keeping it, but sitting in judgment on it. There is only one Lawgiver and Judge, the one who is able to save and destroy. But you—who are you to judge your neighbor?*[5]

Yeah, that.

Step 8: Ask them for prayer.

It's my new strategy when dealing with the people who destroy me for my preaching or my writings. I ask for their prayers, because who knows— maybe they're right about me! Who am I to presume that my thoughts, opinions, and theology are correct…and that they are wrong? Perhaps I need them more than they need me.

Real-life anecdote: a super-religious preacher in Puerto Rico was about to die. He was popular in the church, and for horrible reasons, he was also popular outside of it. He was the guy who sent everyone to hell, and he was proud of it. He did it through screams, shouts, and spits (on national TV), and his passion and consistency made him infamous for years. A few weeks before that preacher went to heaven, another famous, super-prosperity-flashy preacher invited the first to speak at his church. They were literally the polar opposites in every single theological way. They dressed differently, preached differently, acted differently, and sinned differently—but Jesus is a magnet and He brought His iron-sons together.

Everyone was confused by the invitation. The religious preacher had publicly insulted the prosperity preacher (and vice versa) on multiple occasions. In turn, most of the church and the media thought the whole thing was a marketing ploy. But when the religious preacher started to preach, he began to repent. He spoke of misusing the pulpit and hurting the family of God. He was sincere and humble. And at the end of his beautiful sermon the prosperity pastor brought a bucket of water, knelt down, and washed the jerk's feet.

The humble preacher died a few days after, with feet washed in the grace of his prosperous brother.

I would have never visited either of those pastors' churches. They were not my cup of tea. But on that day of repentance and humility, they became a manifestation of Jesus to the world. They showed the goodness of Christ to His body, they demonstrated the power of forgiveness and reconciliation, and they taught me a life-long lesson in decency.

Jesus (as always) said it perfectly: *"I say to you who hear, Love your enemies, do good to those who hate you."*[6] Even if they're part of the Christian family, let's stop looking for a fight. Let's get hungry for connection. Let's wash each other in God's loving grace. And let's take the advice from Brené Brown, who said, quoting her husband, "I'll never know if people are doing the best they can or not. But when I assume they are, it makes my life a lot better."[7]

Notes

1. Bruxy Cavey, *The End of Religion: Encountering the Subversive Spirituality of Jesus* (Colorado Springs: NavPress, 2007), 94.
2. James 1:27 NIV.
3. Luke 9:54–55.

4. Brian Zahnd, Twitter post, April 16, 2015, 8:23 p.m., http://twitter.com/BrianZahnd.

5. James 4:11–12 NIV.

6. Luke 6:27.

7. Quoted in Lisa Richardson, "'I am not as sweet as I used to be, but I am far more loving.' Brené Brown says it's more than okay to have healthy boundaries in place," thewellnessalmanac.com, April 18, 2016, https://thewellnessalmanac.com/2016/04/18/i-am-not-as-sweet-as-i-used-to-be-but-i-am-far-more-loving-brene-brown-says-its-more-than-okay-to-have-healthy-boundaries-in-place/. (Accessed March 25, 2017.)

ACT 2

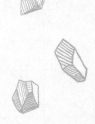

THE WOMAN

*H*e *is so much better than my useless husband,* she thought while biting her lips. Even so, she felt afraid, terrified actually, but she knew that would make for even better sex.

On their third encounter outside the busy market they had decided to go back to his place. She recognized with all of her heart that it was wrong, and yet somehow it was her very heart that was compelling her to go.

His wife was visiting her cousin. Her husband (useless as ever) was away with friends in Capernaum. And everyone in Jerusalem seemed to be distracted by the miracle-worker from Nazareth.

"Tonight?" he asked aggressively for the second time.

Yes, she replied with a nod and her eyes.

Up they went, walking with enough distance between them to pretend like they were not together, but close enough to create an even more exciting tension. As they entered the room she remembered the Song of Solomon. Her new lover's decisiveness was so attractive. She herself felt empowered and in control. Plus, she couldn't get enough of how he looked at her, and how that made her feel alive again. This is what her heart had always wanted, so she whispered under her breath, *"Kiss me with the kisses of* [your] *mouth, for your love is better than wine."*[1]

That same beating heart, now beating faster than ever in the rhythms of pleasure, almost stopped in shock when the door was opened with the force as of a Philistine giant.

A short man with a long beard and a dark hat stepped inside, shaking with anger and eyes bloodshot. "You filthy harlot, you!" he screamed. "I knew my brother was being cheated on! And now there is no doubt!"

The man she was sleeping with stood up, kissed her forehead, and walked naked past her brother-in-law. They winked at each other as if they had planned this all along, and the woman was left fully exposed, naked, and alone.

Two other men entered the room and hauled her out. "I heard you, I saw you, and so did *Yahweh*," the religious leader said decisively. "Now get ready for the rocks."

Terror filled her eyes as she was dragged down to the main street. All too quickly, people began to whisper, and then they began to cheer. It had been a while since they had held a public stoning, but the religious leaders and those gathering seemed primed for it.

"Whore!" screamed her neighbors.

"Slut!" shouted a kid.

The short man held on to her arm and would not relax his grip. "Your parents would be so embarrassed right now, woman," he said with a hint of pleasure. "Thank the heavens they are dead and not around to see your holy execution."

I'll join them soon enough, she thought, as her life flashed before her eyes. The nearness of death was so real that she could barely feel the spits and the pebbles being flung at her. As early as it was, it seemed like all of Jerusalem was already aware of her failure.

Then, she noticed the sunrise. For a second, she decided to take in a deep breath of fresh air. *Maybe my last*, she thought, and with that thought she screamed louder than she had ever screamed before.

As she collapsed again, the woman looked down at her bare breast and realized her heart was almost beating out of her chest. Worst of all, she realized that as she sat in the dirt, she was truly all alone.

Notes

1. Song of Solomon 1:2.

15

BOTH

"There's a reason women flocked to Jesus:
Because he intentionally included & empowered women
when other religious men of influence didn't."[1]
—*Jory Micah*

Let me start Act 2 by highlighting the fact that the woman who was caught in the act of adultery was brought to be stoned alone. The men who were experts at knowing and teaching the law were breaking the law in John 8. This bastion of male chauvinism forgot to follow the full extent of Leviticus 20:10: *"Both the adulterer and the adulteress shall surely be put to death."*

Both.

Unfortunately for the 49.6 percent of the population of the world who are female, discrimination, prejudice, and misogyny are still the norm.

Jesus, on the other hand, used His manhood differently.

His earthly ministry was supported by women, successful ladies who made more money than Jesus and His twelve. They were the ones who provided finances for food and travel,[2] and Jesus had zero issues with that. He had no *macho* pride to hinder it. Actually, women are the only financial supporters mentioned in the Bible by name.

These incredible women did not merely write a check to cover the expenses; they also served meals, preached the good news, healed the sick, and accompanied Jesus.

But there is a lie that still runs through the veins of male-dominated Christianity: *Men are more powerful and God has given them control over the church.*

It's not a new deception.

It's the rape culture in "spiritual" form.

The *rape culture* is a complex set of beliefs and cultural norms that encourage male aggression and support violence against women.[3] This may sound like an exaggeration to some of us guys, but in far too many men, it is the rage that exists deep inside. And as a female friend of mine shared, "I can't imagine finding a woman in this decade who hasn't been propositioned in a way that felt menacing, groped against her will, or even had dirty comments shouted at her as she walked the street."

#NotRight.

As wild as this is to write, we need to understand that Jesus was tempted with this. As a young, single, sought-after speaker, Jesus was faced with thousands of women who approached Him for healing, for attention, and for worship. Some of them were attractive, some desperate, others interesting and engaging, and even one, who was known for her sexual sins, showered Him with oil while kissing His feet (more on her later).

Jesus could have slept with any one of them. He could have forced Himself on them. He surely was tempted to take advantage and speak derisively about them while hanging out with His twelve buddies. The Bible is explicit, "*We do not have a high priest who is unable to empathize with our weaknesses, **but we have one who has been tempted in every way**, just as we are—yet he did not sin.*"[4]

Unfortunately, there are living and breathing examples of church leaders who have used their charisma and power to seduce and abuse women, to devalue and discredit them, to stone them with their words, and to rape them with their gaze (and even worse).

In Jesus' lifetime, Jewish rabbis began every temple meeting with the words "Blessed art thou, O Lord, for Thou hast not made me a woman." However, the perfect Teacher took a different approach.

We read Scripture without realizing that addressing women directly, and in public, was extremely unusual for a Rabbi to do. As Philip Yancey wrote, "For women and other oppressed people, Jesus turned upside down the accepted wisdom of His day…. According to biblical scholar Walter Wink, Jesus violated the mores of His time in every single encounter with women recorded in the four Gospels."[5]

When the woman broke perfume over Jesus' feet and washed them with her hair, or when the woman with the issue of blood touched His robe, or when He took the hand of the dead daughter of Jairus, or when Mary sat at His feet listening to His teaching—whenever those things happened, they defied all the normal rules of society.

And Jesus *is* what God has to say about women.

With His ministry, Jesus taught that women were equal to men in God's eyes, that they could receive forgiveness and grace, that they could be among Christ's personal followers—full participants in the kingdom of God. And these ideas were revolutionary!

They continue to be.

Occasionally, male leaders in the church fight hard to push for the "guidelines" set by the apostle Paul concerning women. Yet at the same time they ignore the incredible legacy Jesus left for the role of a woman with authority in ministry. Paul himself made the most stunning invitation to us (the male husband) to, *"Love your wives, as Christ loved the church and gave himself up for her,"*[6] which is the highest standard and the greatest sacrifice (and the main verse we men need to focus on).

Author Danny Silk is aware, "The church should be the safest, freest, and most empowering place for women, for anyone. But the fact remains that the patriarchal paradigm still exists in the church."[7]

It is ironic that with the low status of women in His day, the first Christian preachers of the resurrection were not men, but women. Jesus did not appear first to Peter, or even the beloved disciple John. He appeared first to Mary, and the other women who followed Him and served Him. Mary, who saw Him first, became the first person ever to let other people know, "He is alive!"—the ultimate message of Christianity. She was the first ambassador of the new covenant. And I believe Jesus deliberately appeared to her first. He was sending the church a message spoken through actions not just words, a message He is still sending today.

I have five strong and beautiful sisters. I was raised by a funny, God-fearing, hard-working mother. My best friend in the world, and wife of eleven years, is a gorgeous, caring, and educated British lady. I have been surrounded by powerful women pastors my whole life, and I am grateful to God for their tenacity and example.

The image of God is incomplete without their compassion, their strength, and their radiance. In the words of Albert Benjamin Simpson, "The heart of Christ is not only the heart of a man but has in it also the tenderness and gentleness of a woman. Jesus was not a man in the rigid sense of manhood as distinct from womanhood, but, as the Son of Man, the complete Head of humanity."[8]

There is a nasty symptom of the rape culture that is still pulsating through media, entertainment, politics, and the family of God. It's time to recognize the temptation to exploit and abuse, and the ungodly desire to control and dominate (I know I have it, and I need women to help me be aware, and to do better).

Of course, I will continue to write about the extravagant grace that is available for abusers, for pedophiles in prison, for abusive husbands, and rapists. *God knows we need it.* But we need to start showing dramatic grace for the victim, the hurting, and the innocent.

It starts with abusers owning their abuse: no excuses, no justifications.

It moves to the victims walking in radical forgiveness: at their pace, with our support.

It ends with the church not hiding its weakness, and taking responsibility for its faults.

Christ is the standard and Christ cares about women's fair wages. He is committed to their honor in leadership. He has given them a platform of influence and transformation. And our homes and churches need to be the safest, most empowering place for all of them.

God the Father wants all rape culture (speech, behavior, and thought) eliminated.

Let's begin with self-awareness.

Let's have the honest conversation.

And boys, let's be the godly men who use our manhood differently.

Notes

1. Jory Micah, Twitter post, December 28, 2016, 8:45 p.m., http://twitter.com/JoryMicah.
2. See Luke 8:3.
3. For more on rape culture: Emilie Buchwald and Pamela R. Fletcher, *Transforming Rape Culture*, edited by Martha Roth (Minneapolis: Milkweed Editions, 1993).
4. Hebrews 4:15 NIV.
5. Phillip Yancey, *The Jesus I Never Knew* (Nashville: Thomas Nelson, 1994), 154.
6. Ephesians 5:25.
7. Danny Silk, *Powerful and Free: Confronting the Glass Ceiling for Women in the Church* (Redding, CA: Red Arrow Publishing, 2013), 27.
8. A. B. Simpson, *When the Comforter Came* (New York: Christian Publications, 1911), 16.

16

WHO ARE YOU TOUCHING?

"Destiny isn't the stuff you're going to do,
it's the people you're going to love."[1]
—*Shawn Bolz*

If you're a bit of a germaphobe—and who isn't (slowly raises hand)—it's hard to comprehend how Jesus could touch so many lepers. The fact that they were called *lepers* seems insulting to me, but they were so marginalized that none of the four Gospels record the name of any of the people who were healed of this terrible disease.

There is one instance in Matthew when the Messiah came down after the Sermon on the Mount and large crowds followed Him. A man full of leprosy came and fell to his knees before Jesus and said, *"Lord, if you will, you can make me clean."*[2] God the Son reached out His hand and touched him. *"I will,"* He said, *"be clean."*[3] Instantly, the man was healed of his leprosy.

> Leprosy is a chronic disease caused by a bacillus: Mycobacterium leprae.... The disease mainly affects the skin, the peripheral nerves, mucosa of the upper respiratory tract, and also the eyes. Leprosy is curable with multidrug therapy (MDT). Although not highly infectious, leprosy is transmitted via droplets, from the nose and mouth, during close and frequent contacts with untreated cases.

Untreated, leprosy can cause progressive and permanent damage to the skin, nerves, limbs, and eyes.[4]

The Law of Moses was clear about what to do with this "abomination." In Leviticus 13, we read the particular procedures required to deal with a person infected with leprosy. A priest would have to examine the lesions, and after a period of observation, if the condition did not improve, the individual would be announced as "infected."

On top of the physical turmoil, leprosy was considered a curse from God of profound impurity. To be declared unclean because of leprosy meant that the outcast would have to tear his clothes, put a covering upon his upper lip, and shout out on the streets, "Unclean! Cursed and unclean!"

Concerned with the contagious nature of the sickness, the Jewish people forced lepers to live completely disconnected and outside the camp. Blacklisted from the community, they were left destitute, without the support of their friends and relatives.

This leper who approached Jesus was breaking the Levitical law. By touching him, Jesus defied the Levitical law even more, proving once again that He was not moved by love of the law, but by the law of love.

When the Christ sent His disciples with instructions to heal the sick, cleansing the lepers was specifically mentioned.[5] Think about this for a second, Jesus was touching the skin of men and women who were melting under the "curse of God." And He tells us to do the same.

Now think about anyone alive who is considered to be "under a curse." From poverty, disability, mental illness, location, culture, or whatever else our ignorance has labeled as *cursed*. Well, who cares what our ungodly theologies have defined as evil, bad, dirty, or damned. According to Emmanuel we are to reach out our hands, touch them, speak to them, and heal them. It is the very act that declares, "God is with us!"

For some of the lepers who came to Jesus, it is quite possible that their greatest healing, even beyond being saved from their disease, was the fact that another human being touched them. After years of separation, distance, and rejection, what would it have felt like to be touched by the warm hand of the Jewish Messiah?

What does it feel like to you?

When you're lonely, sick, or hurting on the inside and someone comes close; when then they show you compassion, scratch your back with friendly tenderness, allow you to contaminate their space with whatever it is that is contaminating yours.

This is the kingdom.

This is the invitation.

It's the basic, obvious, trademark of Jesus.

When is it going to be the basic, obvious, trademark of His people?

Notes

1. Shawn Bolz, "Shawn Bolz Stories – How to Come into Your Destiny: Charles Jones," August 13, 2016, YouTube video, 6:02, https://m.youtube.com/watch?v=1-jVPONcAug.
2. Matthew 8:2.
3. Verse 3.
4. Leprosy Fact Sheet, World Health Organization, updated February 2017, http://www.who.int/mediacentre/factsheets/fs101/en/.
5. See Matthew 10:8.

17

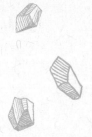

BETTER

"You have not lived today until you have done something for
someone who can never repay you."[1]
—*John Bunyan*

Craig Romkema is one of my favorite poets ever. He's thirty-six, loves
watching basketball, and is an avid fan of geography. I met Craig in 2011
for the first time. And in that first encounter, I spent twenty minutes with
my arms around him, praying. As I prayed, his mom kept telling me how
hard the last few months had been. Craig's father had recently passed away
and she was thinking of moving from Iowa to Raleigh to be closer to family
and to be able to attend our church regularly.

I listened, I smiled, and I kept trying to pray.

But more than anything else about that night, I remember the feeling
of Craig's beard on my fingertips. *How come?* Because Craig lives with the
symptoms of autism and cerebral palsy. He has severe movement disability and is unable to have a one-on-one conversation without monumental
assistance. His most basic point of connection is to grab your hand, put it
on his chin, and say the word *tickle*.

He can comprehend this book, enjoy the new Avengers movie, and
have deep thoughts about history, but he just can't express them. His brain

functions are not that different from ours, but his body and his voice keep him in a prison of being misunderstood.

Imagine living in a country where you understand the language but nobody understands you. Imagine being in love with a person but every time you wanted to kiss them you ended up pushing them away. That's what it's like being Craig.

A few years after those first twenty minutes, Craig's mom was diagnosed with cancer. We tried our absolute best as a church to be there for the family—bringing meals, praying with faith, and hanging out with Craig so his mom could go for her doctor's visits. And that became my Thursday mornings. For weeks, I would pick up Craig and we would hang out together. Yes, there was always something "more important" to do that day…prepare a sermon, answer emails, lead a meeting, write this chapter.

Still, I couldn't shake it. I needed more of Jesus, and spending time with Craig felt like the closest time with Jesus I had every week.

On our third date together things began to get serious. As we were driving along, I noticed that Craig was focused on a car that was about to exit a cheap gas station car wash. I also noticed that my car needed a good cleaning so I sang out loud (in the necessary falsetto), *"At the car wash… woooh! Talking about the car wash, yeah!"*

I looked at my co-pilot, and after three seconds of nothing…Craig lost it.

So I lost it.

We laughed so hard my stomach began to properly hurt. I think I lost three pounds and gained one abdominal muscle. And I understood why Karl Barth wrote, "Laughter is the closest thing to the grace of God."

Just when the moment was about to pass, I felt compelled to sing it again, loud and proud, *"At the car wash…woooh! Talking about the car wash, yeah!"*

I'm pretty sure that's the most I have ever laughed with another human being in a twenty minute stretch. Craig peed himself a little, and so did I.

I'm also pretty sure that's the most I have ever enjoyed God's presence while singing a song in my car (sorry Hillsong).

Of course, we went straight to the car wash singing the song over and over again. *You guessed it,* Craig started singing with me! I would start with, "At the car wash"…and he would add the sound effects.

Me: *"Talking about the car wash"* (Still in falsetto)

Craig: *"ye-ah!"* (In his beautiful, raspy, barely-understandable voice.)

For weeks and weeks my car was the cleanest vehicle in the state. Every Thursday morning I would pick up Craig, grab him a cup of decaffeinated coffee, read him Pablo Neruda poems inside Barnes and Noble, and then we would head over to the car wash.

Singing.

My dad has a saying that he picked up from my *abuelo*: "Things that are done well, look well." My mom also has a saying, which she told us on a weekly basis (in full mom-tone): "Life will teach you." I can imagine you have a few of your own—you probably picked them up from a grandparent or an old boss.

Jesus Christ had a saying. It was the sort of quote that people heard, remembered, and shared (his most tweet-able line). And yet it did not make it into the four Gospels. We hear it via the apostle Paul, while he's speaking to a group of church leaders. He's telling them about an upcoming, dangerous trip. He's also reminding them to take care of God's flock and to have no desire for wealth or fancy robes. And his whole sermon is built on that famous echo, "It is better to give than to receive." As in, *"In all things I have shown you that by working hard in this way we must help the weak and remember the words of the Lord Jesus, how he himself said,* **'It is more blessed to give than to receive.'"**[2]

The system of this world cannot understand that concept intellectually; it can only be experienced with the heart.

Notice that Paul is not telling unbelievers to try this—he is speaking to church leaders. It's a reminder to those in authority of the ultimate roar from heaven. The style of the kingdom, giving not taking, loving not drawing, providing not withholding.

I must say that giving my time, my money, and my social energy to Craig was one of the best investments I have ever made to myself.

My charity became my pleasure.

The car wash became the church.

My brother became my savior.

The man I was trying to help became a friend that helped me focus. I rediscovered the joy of friendship during my time with Craig. It was beautifully awkward to walk around the nicest mall in Durham, North Carolina, with a grown man resting my hand against his beard and asking me to tickle him again.

Looking into my brother's eyes made me realize how little I was looking into myself. Through his harsh voice and his broken walk, he showed me time and time again that a person with a disability has the ability to overcome the worst. Everyday. At every moment. On the family's GoFundMe page, this is written about Craig: "A pioneer throughout his life, Craig has been the first with this disability to attend his local elementary school, to graduate with honors from his high school, and, after ten years of hard work, to receive his degree in English Literature from Dordt College."[3] *What a champion!*

Trust me, I have prayed many times for Craig to be healed—I still do. I wrestle with God because my friend is not well, and God could make him well. I know He can. However, while I wait for the miracle, I hang out with my brother. I love my brother where he is; I do whatever it takes to connect with him, to show him that he matters, that his life is valuable.

I like how Bob Goff said it: "Give away time and you'll find empathy; give away empathy and you'll find love; give away love and you'll find purpose. Keep trading up."[4]

When Craig's beautiful mother passed away, I had the privilege of preaching at her funeral. There were no words to make the moment easier. I just shared the good news of Jesus because I knew that is exactly what she would have wanted her family to listen to. After reading Scripture, praying for the family, and watching a slideshow of Craig's mom with all the relatives, we gathered for snacks and sweets.

I wanted to provide comfort. I wanted to pastor the moment well. But the only thing I could offer to Craig at the funeral was a look into his eyes and the sound of our song: *"At the car wash, yeah!"* With tears and smiles on our faces, we sang it with others. It was a human moment; a sweet, awkward moment among friends. And it was the kind of giving that is expecting nothing in return.

I agree with Jesus, it was better.

Notes

1. John Bunyan quoted in James Lloyd, *Torch Tips for a Luminous Life* (Newbury Park, CA: 9 Screens International, 2006), 75.
2. Acts 20:35.
3. "Story," https://www.gofundme.com/barbandcraig. (Accessed June 23, 2017.)
4. Bob Goff, Twitter post, December 10, 2016, 12:55 p.m., http://twitter.com/bobgoff.

18

THE ART OF JUDGMENTAL THINKING

"If you believe what you like in the gospels, and reject what you
don't like, it is not the gospel you believe, but yourself."
—*attributed to Saint Augustine*

Adultery is a major sin. It's a destructive malice that corrupts the sanctity of marriage. But it's just one of the 677 major sins in the Bible. It goes from selfishness, to fornication, to murder, to gossip, to being double-minded… so it is clear that we are all sinful (and even more clear that we need redemption). The law proves that we are imperfect; the gospel provides a perfect Savior.

Yes, we are God's children, a royal priesthood, adopted and beloved, the apple of His eye, but the apostle Paul carried a beautiful tension that we can all learn from. He went from calling himself "chief sinner"[1] to telling people to *"be imitators of me, as I am of Christ."*[2] He displayed his authority as a great missionary, while at the same time displaying the struggles of his human flesh. He was a man who understood his great calling as "Paul," while simultaneously embracing his great frailty as "Saul."

We could use a little bit more of this tension in the church. It's either too much about *me and my greatness* or too much about *them and their wickedness*. What would happen if we focused on the beauty of others while dealing with the transgressions of self? This is not about being soft on sin;

this is more about the unbalance of being soft with our sins and tough on theirs.

I don't think the world is put off by the church's weakness, but rather by its fakeness. So what if the main thing we highlighted was our need for Jesus instead of the world's need for us?

I have a friend in Texas who throws the most extravagant baby showers for girls who have unplanned pregnancies. And when I say extravagant, I mean *Texas extravagant.*

Her name is Amy Ford and her ministry, Embrace Grace, is now in hundreds of churches all across the United States. At nineteen years old, Amy went through the trauma of being rejected because of her unplanned pregnancy. She fainted moments before her abortion was to take place, and even though she chose life, and even though she chose to marry the father of her child, her Christian friends and leaders still rejected her. The shame she carried was almost unbearable, yet she decided to trust God and raise her baby boy in love. Then she resolved to break the shame cycle and start a program in which young ladies could experience the joy of their miracle in ways she was never able to.

People have criticized their ministry for "encouraging sinful behavior" but Amy and her team have embraced the opportunity to celebrate new life and preach the story of redemption—one shower at a time.

I know biblically why Amy loves so much: it's because she's been forgiven much.

One time, Jesus was invited to a dinner party hosted by a Pharisee named Simon. A woman of the city, who was a known prostitute, fell to her knees and cried at the feet of the Holy Man. While everyone was looking, she poured out the most expensive oil, used her own hair as washcloth, and kissed the feet of Christ in adoration. "[The religious host] *said to himself, 'If this man was the prophet I thought he was, he would have known what kind of woman this is who is falling all over him.'"*[3]

Jesus, knowing Simon's inner thoughts, answered him with the short parable: *"Two men were in debt to a banker. One owed five hundred silver pieces, the other fifty. Neither of them could pay up, and so the banker canceled both debts. Which of the two would be more grateful?"*

Simon answered, "I suppose the one who was forgiven the most."[4]

Demolishing every norm that existed, Jesus told Simon to learn from the worshipping prostitute, not the other way around.

"That's right," said Jesus. Then turning to the woman, but speaking to Simon, he said, "Do you see this woman? I came to your home; you provided no water for my feet, but she rained tears on my feet and dried them with her hair. You gave me no greeting, but from the time I arrived she hasn't quit kissing my feet. You provided nothing for freshening up, but she has soothed my feet with perfume. Impressive, isn't it?"[5]

Then, allow me to switch Bible versions as Jesus finishes His radical declaration with, *"Therefore I tell you, her sins, which are many, are forgiven—for she loved much. But he who is forgiven little, loves little."*[6]

I don't think for a moment Jesus was implying that the woman was more sinful (in quantity or quality) than the men in the room. It was only that her sins were more obvious, out in the open, and easier to define. We know from reading Matthew 23 that Jesus exposed and defined the sins of the Pharisees themselves, and that would have been the point. If you think you only struggle with a few things, then you will only be grateful for a few things. If you're aware of the many transgressions that consume you, then many will be your worship songs at the feet of the Savior.

I'm not talking about glorifying our transgressions; I'm talking about being accurately aware of the many times God has forgiven us and loved us through them.

There are 677 sins in the Bible. Whether you struggle with only one of them or 676 of them, *"the wages of sin is death."*[7] Notice that *"sin"* is singular.

Just one is enough.

Judging a person who has three hundred visible sins does not deal with the three that you're hiding. That is why the art of judgmental thinking needs to be replaced with the beauty of awareness and gratitude, just like Amy Ford did in her life. She fell at the feet of Jesus, received His words of grace (for her life and child), and now lives that out for others.

Her story of rejection became the invitation. The love that she received became her motivation. What the enemy intended for evil, Jesus and Amy turned around for good.

Tag, you're it.

Notes
1. See 1 Timothy 1:15 NKJV.
2. 1 Corinthians 11:1.
3. Luke 7:39 MSG.
4. Verses 41–43 MSG.
5. Verses 44–46 MSG.
6. Luke 7:47.
7. Romans 6:23.

19

POP CULTURE GOSPEL

"God doesn't share our rating system. To him, all sin is equally
evil, and all sinners are equally lovable."[1]
—*Judah Smith*

Finding myself as the woman in the story, caught in the act of
_____ (choose one of my many sins from the previous chapters) helped me refocus my attention.

So I began to write.

Writing became my processing station, a cheaper, less effective version of counseling. I took the advice of my friend and started a blog called HappySonship.com. I was pursuing the branding of the word *Sonship* but failed to make that happen. You see, in my charismatic/father heart circles, *sonship* is Mecca. It's where we want everybody to get to. I tried buying the actual domain sonship.com, but twenty thousand dollars seemed a tad high for my budget (just a tad). I went with the more appropriate $3.95 a month and choose the domain HappySonship.com.

This all happened during that terrible summer when the song "Happy" by Pharrell dominated the airwaves. Yes, the same summer when actual sadness was dominating my air and my waves. Still, my sons (and most of America) did not want to listen to anything else but the pop hit single from *Despicable Me 2*.

There were only a few happy moments throughout that whole season for me. Yet, in the middle of it, my intuitive wife had a dream that something significant would happen on an insignificant date. And it was on October 3, when I learned about blogging and launched my website to the Internet. Truth is, I did not think starting a blog would be a significant part of my life (at least not a *God-giving-a-date-in-a-dream* kind of significant thing). Yet what happened next altered everything.

The first few posts on the blog were all about letting people know that even when life sucks, God's love doesn't. My goal in sharing was to be as transparent as possible and test people's reaction to it. To my surprise, more than four million unique visitors came to the site in the first year. All I was doing was writing short articles with headlines like: "The 20 Worst Mistakes I've Made as a Pastor," "The Ultimate Guide for First-Time Christian Sex," and "What to Do When You're Hurting." And they were all written with a combination of humor, pain, and authenticity.

One specific night, I decided to comment on the "born again" experience of Hollywood superstar Shia LaBeouf. After filming the WWII drama *Fury*, in which he played a Christian man nicknamed "Bible," Shia told *Interview* magazine,

> I found God doing Fury. I became a Christian man, and not in a f***ing bull***t way—in a very real way. I could have just said the prayers that were on the page. But it was a real thing that really saved me. And you can't identify unless you're really going through it. It's a full-blown exchange of heart, a surrender of control.[2]

I wrote seven-hundred-plus words about how Jesus hung out with sinners, had a few cursing men as His followers, and how Brother LaBeouf would fit perfectly with them. In less than three days, more than two hundred and fifty thousand people had read the article. But it was not the numbers that impressed me. It was the comments that ranged from "How refreshing that someone is saying this!" to "Hey, charlatan, this is absolute heresy!"

The first group made me nervous; it made me wonder, *Wait, no one else is saying this?* The second group mostly confirmed a lot of what I had been hearing and seeing in my six years of pastoring in the Christian South.

And because of it, I wrote some more.

For a while, it was mostly a grace response to whatever was trending in social media. When people were complaining about Obama, I wrote about praying for your leaders. When people were condemning a pastor who had fallen in sin, I wrote about my failings and the compassion of Jesus. When people were sending Bruce Jenner to hell for coming out as Caitlyn Jenner, I wrote about Jesus inviting the religious leaders to drop the stones.

That last one was the article that started the journey of this book.

It was titled "How God Looks at Bruce Jenner." More than a 1.2 million individuals read that article in a few days and I received hundreds of calls and emails from people all across the globe. During the week, the article went viral, and I discovered something: the people who preach grace are mostly afraid, the people who sermonize judgments are mostly bold, and the equation needed to change. I found thousands of believers in the Jesus way, who kept those ways a secret. I was simultaneously attacked by hundreds of believers in the name of Jesus. They insulted me, declared me lost, and one even accused me of being part of the Illuminati.

Yes, *the Illuminati.*

And there was one more crowd, a sharp, more cautious flock. These were the sons and daughters of Christian parents who were struggling with their faith. Some asked to meet with me. Others wrote me letters of appreciation, while confessing their struggles with homosexuality, doubting God's existence, and/or loving to smoke weed. I realized that there is a church within the church that is alive yet broken. They have endured years of religious leaders' agendas and the hope of Christ is all but gone.

I blog for them, knowing that caring for people the way Jesus did means a life of being misinterpreted.

The Pew Research Center released a survey of 35,000 American adults that showed that the Christian percentage of the population was dropping precipitously, to 70.6 percent.[3] Daniel Burke of CNN reported,

In 2007, 78.4% of American adults called themselves Christian. In the meantime, almost every major branch of Christianity in the United States has lost a significant number of members, mainly because millennials are leaving the fold. More than one-third of millennials now say they are unaffiliated with any faith, up ten percentage points since 2007. The alacrity of their exodus surprises even seasoned experts. "We've known that the religiously unaffiliated has been growing for decades," said Greg Smith, Pew's associate director of religion research and the lead researcher on the new study. "But the pace at which they've continued to grow is really astounding." It's not just millennials leaving the church. Whether married or single, rich or poor, young or old, living in the West or the Bible Belt, almost every demographic group has seen a significant drop in people who call themselves Christians, Pew found.[4]

Can you blame them?

It seems like the love triangle between politics, religion, and Christianity has produced a faith that keeps people out instead of loving them in. Vocal Christian leaders highlight the sins of Hollywood and liberals while ignoring the sins of the church. We fight publicly, criticize publicly, and complain publicly, all while forgetting that the Lord said (publicly), *"Those who are well have no need of a physician, but those who are sick. I came not to call the righteous, but sinners."*[5]

Nothing reaches people like being loved when they least deserve it; and nothing pushes people away like being judged when they don't.

I know Western Christianity is losing people.

But Christ isn't.

Here's our chance to join Him.

Notes

1. Judah Smith, *Jesus Is _____: Find a New Way to Be Human* (Nashville: Thomas Nelson, 2013), 4–5.
2. Elvis Mitchell, "Shia LaBeouf," *Interview*, October 20, 2014, http://www.interviewmagazine.com/film/shia-labeouf#page2. (Accessed March 26, 2017.)
3. Pew Forum on Religion and Public Life, *Global Christianity: A Report on the Size and Distribution of the World's Christian Population* (Pew Research Center, 2011), 67.
4. Daniel Burke, "Millenials leaving church in droves, study finds," *CNN.com*, May 14, 2015, http://www.cnn.com/2015/05/12/living/pew-religion-study/. (Accessed March 26, 2017.)
5. Mark 2:17.

20

REFOCUSING OUR ATTENTION

"The gospel isn't just for abortionists prostitutes
homosexuals but for porn-addicted pastors unconverted
elders and self-righteous churchgoers."[1]
—*Burk Parsons*

The church has done a good job at making John 3:16 a well-known verse. I'm so confident in your familiarity with it, that I won't even make it available on this page. But right after John 3:16, comes John 3:17. And this verse, which deserves as much attention as the previous one, demands a thorough read: *"For God did not send his Son into the world to condemn the world, but in order that the world might be saved through him."*

This is God's intention, His desire, and His labor. It's clear, precise, and available. Jesus did not come to condemn the world; He came to save it. The same language is used in the story of John 8:11, when Jesus said, *"Neither do I condemn you."*

So, what is God's plan with the transgender or the homosexual?

Salvation.

And in the way of Christ, salvation starts with friendship.

Since I was ordained as a pastor in 2004 I have officiated more than fifty weddings. I have officiated the weddings of my three best friends, and

I have done quick ceremonies because someone got "knocked up." I have done weddings in which I was asked not to use the name of Jesus, and weddings where they asked me to preach the gospel like we were in an evangelistic crusade (with altar call and deliverance). I served each couple as best as I could. Their wedding day was their wedding day, so I accommodated to give them the experience they wanted, without forgetting who I was.

And I did my job without judging them for being fornicators, divorcées, liars, or cheap (ok, maybe I judged a little).

Yet after the Supreme Court legalized same-sex marriage in the US, I had to ask myself, *would I do a same-sex wedding?*

In a landmark opinion, a divided Supreme Court ruled that states cannot ban same-sex marriage, establishing a new civil right and handing same-sex rights advocates a victory that until very recently seemed unthinkable. The possibility exists for me to either get in trouble with the law for denying a homosexual couple the right to get married (not that it is written like this currently) or to face backlash in the church for actually doing the wedding.

It might be obvious to you what I should do.

But I have a few thoughts on both sides of the debate.

As Carl Medearis said,

Truth and Grace. A fine balancing act. No bumper sticker answers. No easy black and white responses to complicated questions involving real live human beings made in the image of God who are desperately seeking to find him.[2]

Gay marriage is now the law of the land. And who knows? Maybe because we are not reaching out with love, hope, and grace to the LGBTQ community, God is bringing them to us. And now that we can't keep them at a "safe" distance, we will have to engage.

History has taught us this lesson over and over again: laws don't change people's hearts, only the Spirit does.

As a Christian pastor, the decision of the Supreme Court might affect my ministry, my livelihood, and my core beliefs. Other people in America were celebrating, and even while I don't completely agree with the redefinition of marriage, I understand it. Whether they're right or wrong, denying gays and lesbians the right to get married feels to them like I would feel if a Puerto Rican man was denied the right to marry a British woman—which is my reality, and my right.

Also, the majority of US citizens agree with the decision of the Supreme Court, not with the church's view. And although a good portion of the body of Christ has been fighting with politics, prayer, and civil action in trying to reverse the trend, our culture is not changed by rules or morals or behavior modification.

It takes love.

It takes sacrifice.

It takes the cross.

Maybe we could pivot to the actual work of the gospel. Now that we have "lost" this moral fight, we can start focusing on the hearts of men. The money that was invested on saying "no" to same-sex marriage can now go to feeding the poor, to adoption and foster care, to caring for the elderly, and to taking the good news all across the earth. Maybe this is God's way of redirecting our attention, because we keep trying to change the perception of the world about itself when Jesus is all about changing the world's perception about God's love and God's kingdom.

And I want to join Him in that.

Jesus did not preach, "Repent, because you live in the kingdom of darkness." He declared, *"Repent, for the kingdom of heaven is at hand."*[3]

Even today.

Probably more so today.

"The law came in to increase the trespass, but where sin increased, grace abounded all the more."[4] We seemed more interested in proving how Christian America is, but Christ Himself seemed to be more interested in demonstrating to the citizens of this world how much He loved us, and why He gave Himself for all. The sinless One was never concerned with being seen as the sinless one. He was way more concerned with being a friend to us, the always-sinful ones.

Yes, I don't have to agree with my homosexual friends. Actually, I don't agree with most of my friends on a lot of things. Heck, I don't agree with my wife on a ton of things! That has not stopped me from loving them, supporting them, and being there for them, even when I disagree.

Will I ever officiate the wedding ceremony of a homosexual friend? Probably not. As a pastor I stand by the traditional views of marriage between a man and a woman. I love marriage; I believe in it; and I believe in the One who established it. And my homosexual friends who know this about me love me despite it.

Will I ever be part of the wedding ceremony of one of those friends? Probably yes. I want to be like Jesus, a friend of sinners (and I'm sure He's a friend of sinners, because He's a friend to me). And I'm also sure the wedding where He turned water into wine was full of sinners who needed Him. *Like you and me.*

Perhaps, because of this massive cultural shift, we can stop fighting about what the government will do or won't do about same-sex marriage. Maybe now we can actually engage the LGBTQ community and start working toward honor and understanding. Maybe now the church will stop pretending like it's winning and it can be humble again, servants again, and lovers again. Now we can stop trying to get the world to acknowledge its sin, because the most beautiful thing is when we acknowledge our own—and God is into beautiful things.

Mark Galli wrote in *Christianity Today,*

What actions and attitudes have we imbibed that contribute to our culture's dismissing our ethics? Our homophobia has revealed our fear and prejudice. Biblical inconsistency—our passion to root out sexual sins while relatively indifferent to racism, gluttony, and other sins—opens us to the charge of hypocrisy. Before we spend too much more time trying to straighten out the American neighborhood, we might get our own house in order.[5]

The followers of Jesus were persecuted because they healed the sick, took care of widows, shared all their possessions, and preached the message of Jesus, which is redemption for all and an aberration to the ways of

Caesar. If we continue to be "persecuted" because we defend the phrase "Merry Christmas," or because we say "no" to performing same-sex weddings, then when are we going to be persecuted for actually loving the world, for challenging religious systems, and for demonstrating the kingdom of God? You know, the way of the New Testament.

The church was always meant to be countercultural. Let's just make sure that we are being countercultural because we're aligning with the culture of heaven, not the culture of whatever brand of Christianity we prefer.

I have seen incredible love, conviction, and revelation inside maximum security prisons. I have preached in public high schools and have seen classrooms turned into revival centers. What if a same-sex wedding is next? I could get in trouble for saying no to doing a same-sex wedding *or*, while I'm there, I could witness the hand of God move, with healing, signs, and wonders—where the hearts of the fathers return to their children and the hearts of the children return to their fathers.

I don't know.

I've never seen it.

Maybe it's time to try.

Maybe.

Yes, I'm confused. Yes, I'm trying to navigate grace and truth. Yes, I have no clue what's next. But one thing I know for certain is this: God is in charge and He is very, very good. I know this conversation creates an impossible balance. But we will have to figure it out. And I choose to start with the simplest (most Christian) of steps: forgiveness and blessing.

To the LGBTQ community I say, "I'm sorry for the hatred, the vitriol, and the rejection. There are millions of us Christians who love you and believe God's best for you. We might not see eye to eye, but we promise to love you as Jesus loves us. Help us understand."

With the church I pray, "We bless the Supreme Court, we bless the president, and we bless all of our homosexual friends. We bless the churches that will stand against same-sex rights and the ones that will defend it."

And above all else, "I bless You, Jesus, because You paid the price for us to become part of Your family."

If the homosexual agenda has prevailed today, then it might be the perfect invitation for the grace agenda to start tomorrow. Let's save the energy of hate and use it for love. Let's learn to talk with the marginalized, to try to understand their journey and make their healing our own. Forty-five percent of transgender teens attempt suicide. I don't comprehend their inner torment, but they're not making this up. I don't want to judge them.

Do you?

Notes

1. Burk Parsons, Twitter post, November 16, 2016, 7:40 p.m., http//twitter.com/BurkParsons.
2. Carl Madearis, "Terrorists, Gay Weddings, and the Confederate Flag," *Making Jesus Accessible* (blog), http://carlmedearis.com/2015/06/terrorists-gay-weddings-and-the-confederate-flag/.
3. Matthew 4:17.
4. Romans 5:20.
5. Mark Galli, "Six Things To Do after the Supreme Court Decision on Gay Marriage," *Christianity Today*, June 26, 2015, http://www.christianitytoday.com/ct/2015/june-web-only/6-things-to-do-after-supreme-court-gay-marriage-decision.html. (Accessed March 29, 2017.)

21

RIDICULOUS

"The slender capacity of man's heart cannot
comprehend and much less utter—that unfathomable
depth and burning zeal of God's love toward us."[1]
—*Martin Luther*

He had teardrops tattooed all over his face, some representing a successful murder and others representing being raped in jail. And he was standing in front of me, so close that I could count each and every one of them.

In 2012 I was visiting the city of eternal spring, Medellin, Colombia, and preaching in its biggest church. It was the end of a conference weekend and I had preached in more than ten sessions in less than three days. I was cranky and tired, and ready to eat more plantains.

Visiting Medellin is one of the highlights of my year. The church that hosts me, Comunidad Cristiana de Fe, is one of the most inspiring places on earth. They have thousands of people attending their multiple weekend services. They have loud and passionate worship filling the auditorium, and even louder, more passionate Colombians singing alongside with them. It's not that they are a megachurch, it's the fact that they feel like a family; a humongous, fun-loving, ready-to-take-the-world-for-Jesus kind of a family.

At the end of my last session, after praying and talking with hundreds of people, the hitman approached me crying.

He told me the story of his life, how abuse in his home led to finding safety in a gang, and how his criminal family turned him into a *sicario* (assassin) before he was even a man. He told me that he had been involved in more murders than he could count and how the drug cartels wanted to keep him because of his accuracy and cold-heartedness. Yet throughout the weekend he had heard me preaching on the love of God and his heart was melting in the furnace of grace. In most of my sessions I shared how Jesus came to reveal the father of Luke 15, a father who runs to the prodigal, kisses the prodigal, embraces the prodigal, and then publicly celebrates the returned prodigal. Whenever I preach this story, I deliberately choose a man from the crowd to reenact the action-filled scene. I ask them to go to the furthest point of whatever room we're in. Then I shout Luke 15:20: *"But while he was still a long way off, his father saw him and felt compassion, and ran and embraced him and kissed him."* I then wildly run toward the acting prodigal to hug him and smooch him, profusely.

The assassin in attendance had watched this reenactment in my last sermon and had not stopped crying since. But I was *so* ready to have dinner and go back to the hotel room. I was even more ready to have a late siesta and enjoy the victories of the weekend. I was not ready for what happened next.

While he was still telling me the story of his past, I interrupted him without asking and began to kiss the teardrops on his face. I have no clue what came over me, I just had to kiss him, and them. He cried harder and harder and harder, and then collapsed on the floor. He might have fallen to escape the kisses of the thirty-one-year-old Puerto Rican preacher, but it looked like more than an escape; it looked like surrender.

Then, his two young daughters came running toward him as he lay on the floor. They sat next to him and laid their hands on his chest. They were praying beautiful things like, "God, thank You for our *papito*," "Thank You for forgiving him," "Thank You for his freedom."

I started bawling; I lost myself in the moment and realized that this killer had stolen this experience from so many other people. I realized that others could not cry with their daughters because of his crimes. That they could not attend a church and raise their hands up high to celebrate God's care and provision. Yet here was Jesus, tricking me into kissing the representation of this man's worst, as if to tell him beyond a shadow of a doubt, you are clean and you are forgiven.

For a long time I stood there, watching the trinity of redemption before me. And there I was reminded again of the ridiculousness of grace.

Jesus died for the sins of this man. Jesus died for the sins of the woman caught in adultery. He died so they could live (even though they had destroyed the lives of others). Grace is not just ridiculous, it's unfair—but somehow the righteous Judge makes it work. Like the Bible says, *"For the grace of God has appeared, bringing salvation for all people."*[2]

For you.

For me.

For them.

So (beautifully) unfair.

Notes

1. Quoted in Roland H. Bainton, *Here I Stand* (Nashville: Abingdon Press, 1950), 223.
2. Titus 2:11.

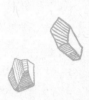

22

PLAGUES OF SELF-HATRED

"You were saved when you believed in Jesus,
but you were transformed when you
realized He believed in you."[1]
—*Kris Vallotton*

We've become experts at judging others because we've had so much internal practice. It's usually in those times of self-hatred when we deliver the kind of hostility that devalues and demonizes others.

The ways of stoning begin in a heart that has turned to stone. And this is the part where I tell you that you are radically loved, because if you miss that, there is no way you can radically love.

Sometimes the most critical people look like the most confident people. Yet, if you look deep inside and get to the core of who they think they are, their confidence is a façade that hides wounds and lies. Self-loathing is their real epidemic, and the cure is not self-love, but a revelation of the Lover above.

King David wrote a well-known psalm that declares a well-known statement. He said this about himself, while talking to the God of the universe: *"For you formed my inward parts; you knitted me together in my mother's womb. I praise you, for I am fearfully and wonderfully made. Wonderful are your works; my soul knows it very well."*[2]

The first point of this psalm is that God is such a phenomenal Creator and Father, and that He made you extravagantly wonderful, distinguished, lovely, superb, delightful, sublime, and mysterious (and the extra adjectives were added because your amazingness, your glory, and your beauty required them).

The second point is that the psalmist knew this as a fact, and accepted these facts as the truth.

"Wonderful are your works," i.e., "Me!"

"My soul knows it very well," i.e., "I'm so confident about my awesomeness that I'm writing a song about it."

This giant-slayer turned monarch was a broken man who knew rejection. He was acquainted with failure and loss. Yes, David was aware of the bad and the ugly in his life, yet he still knew at a soul level that he mattered, and that he was loved.

Loving yourself seems to contradict the very essence of this book—and God knows that we need less books/preaching/conferences on self-love and more books/preaching/conferences on serving others. But we are currently living in the most depressed generation in all of human history. More teenagers are committing suicide than at any other time. It is possible that selfishness and the inability to develop meaningful relationships have much to do with it, but we can't forget the power of words. Life and death is in the tongue;[3] and the tongue of God is full of life for us.

We are invited to be self-aware, not self-critical; we are called to introspection, not intro-rejection, because the hope of the Father is for our future. The very Spirit of God has made us His temple. Jesus not only loves us, but believes in us and endures with us—and people need to know that.

Especially you, my friend.

For the ones who pretend like they have it all together and for the ones who know to a fault that they don't, these next five seconds are for you. Say this out loud:

"Wonderful are your works" i.e., me.

"My soul knows it very well" i.e., I will stop self-stoning and believe what the Father tells me.

Selah.

Notes

1. Kris Vallotton, Twitter post, December 12, 2016, 9:00 a.m., http://twitter.com/kyministries.
2. Psalm 139:13–14.
3. See Proverbs 18:21.

23

ONE MORE TIME

"Freedom flows from knowing your slate is clean, your God
approves, and the fight for acceptance is over."[1]
—*Tullian Tchividjian*

Repetition helps. And in this very important matter, repetition is indispensable.

So stay with me, because I have to tell you one more time that you are majestic; created in beauty and wonder and brimming with the essence of heaven. I have to remind you that you matter, that your voice and desires are a gift not a burden. And I have to address you (in full Pentecostal style) to declare, "*The devil is a liar!*" And whatever he's saying to you is a fabrication worth denying.

The main thing the enemy is trying to do is accuse you, condemn you, and father you. His voice is like that of a religious leader: legalistic, slightly biblical, and daringly convincing. His main purpose is to corrupt the name that God has given you, and to make you question the sincerity of God's caring.

But there is another voice speaking. You can hear it deep in your gut. It's the same voice that initiated you, that sang your fingerprints into being, and that still counts the hairs on your head. It is love Himself, and in the presence of accusation, He speaks again.

Actually, He shouts!

Loudly.

Sincerely.

Right now.

"I'm proud of you and I love you!"

It's your turn now, child. Wake up to the aroma of grace. This very moment is the morning in which God's mercies are new; for you—for this season, and for a lifetime.

I'm not even trying to make you feel better…I'm preaching the gospel truth. This is the message that Jesus came to preach; this is good news to the desolate, to the ones who have been lied to. You are the woman caught in the act of adultery…and here comes Messiah to save you from the stoning.

Here is God, meeting your breathtaking heartache with life-giving tenderness, encountering the faults in you with the luscious goodness in Him, merging your sad story into His glorious future, and proving once again that He is a master of redemption and kindness.

The Son, Jesus, who is now your Brother, approaches you to show you that the Father comes, has come, and will continue to come. And in the coming, He will comfort you like a mother. You are included in the family of all families, the family in which parties have nothing to do with achievements and everything to do with belonging—the place where you are fed, cradled, held, and celebrated.

This is where I tell you one last time that you are majestic. And as royalty, you can make the decree to excommunicate the deceptions and the fear that keep you crawling through the mud of despair. You can call out to the heavens and welcome God's kingdom into your earth, and you can raise your voice boldly to say, "Shut up, shame! I belong to honor. *I am* majestic. And when Christ Jesus asks me, 'Where are they? Has on one condemned you?' I will reply to Him, while thinking of you, 'No one, Lord.'"

"No one."

Now, take a deep breath and read this verse from John, which will help us transition into the next chapter:

In this the love of God was made manifest among us, that God sent his only Son into the world, so that we might live through him. In this is love, not that we have loved God but that he loved us and sent his Son to be the propitiation for our sins.[2]

Notes

1. Tullian Tchividjian, Twitter post, April 21, 2015, 12:17 p.m., http://twitter.com/TullianT.
2. 1 John 4:9–11.

24

WHATEVER YOU NEED TO DO

"Compassion constitutes a radical form of criticism, for it announces that the hurt is to be taken seriously, that the hurt is not to be accepted as normal and natural but is an abnormal and unacceptable condition for humanness."[1]
—*Walter Brueggemann*

A life free from stoning starts with the mouth. A mouth free from stoning starts in the heart. And a heart free from stoning starts in the past. I'm compelled then to ask you, what happened? Who hurt you so badly that your heart now assumes the worst of others? Who broke your trust and stole your encouraging outlook?

For me, it was a combination of childhood trauma, unattended anger, and a theology that was corrupted by self-hatred. You've read already about how that manifested (and there were many more things that did not find its way into these pages). A combination of visible sins plus hidden ones created an atomic bomb that needed to be defused. So I had to fully accept that there were things in me that needed to be attended to before I exploded and destroyed the things that mattered most.

As James Baldwin brilliantly wrote, "I imagine one of the reasons people cling to their hates so stubbornly is because they sense, once hate is gone, they will be forced to deal with pain."[2]

Pastors are not meant to get therapy vs. pastors really need to get therapy. I used to live by statement number one, which is probably why I ended up living statement number two.

Let me start by saying that I am still a pastor, I still believe in the absolute power of Jesus to heal the heart, and I'm still a huge supporter of church counseling and ministry. But I feel compelled to raise my voice and say, "Therapy is not demonic; taking antidepressants is not a sin; seeing a psychiatrist is not anti-Christian; and those who suffer from mental health problems are not a failure."

The Lord knows we need more openness in our congregations because (and this is a fact) 50 percent of adults will develop depression, PTSD, anxiety, self-harming behavior, eating disorders, bipolar disorder, schizophrenia, borderline personality disorder, or some other mental illness in their lifetime.

Half of the people reading this chapter already have—and for the sake of our family, friends, and church leaders, we need to break the shame. Jesus is the hope for each and every one of our needs. He's the Miracle-worker who healed *"every disease and every affliction."*[3] And when Jesus healed the leper, the demon-possessed, or the broken-hearted, He never blamed them for their condition. Jesus is not a religious leader who condemns us if we seek help, Jesus is the High Priest who understands our weaknesses.

"My soul is overwhelmed with sorrow to the point of death." Yes, that was Jesus talking about Himself in Mark 14:34 (NIV). He knows how it feels.

To talk of a person's mental illness like it is the result of a sin, a curse, or demon possession is to further stigmatize, shame, and isolate those who are struggling. It is throwing stones at people who need understanding and a helping hand. Yes, it is possible that sin, curses, and demons are part of the issue, but we need to focus on the person and admit that we don't have all the tools or all the answers for the different situations that need attention.

The church is the place many turn to when in crisis. We cannot keep turning away the most vulnerable among us. We have to learn how to approach and relate to their specific needs. As Brandon Peach wrote,

Most churches probably have the very best intentions when dealing with issues of mental illness. Like the rest of society, however, the church may misinterpret these clinical conditions and respond to them in ways that exacerbate them—and as a result, demoralize those suffering. Christ, the Great Physician, came to heal the sick. As His body, it's time the church leads society in helping to do the same.[4]

I write this chapter not as a pastor, a doctor, or a trained counselor...I approach this subject mostly as a past patient.

A few years ago I needed to visit a psychiatrist to talk about my depression. It was the first time in my life when I actually felt helpless, totally unmotivated, and okay with the idea of suicide. Being able to talk to a professional who could specifically diagnose me and recommend treatment was liberating. Actually, in that moment, it was the godliest thing I could do.

However, I also needed friends who listened. I needed my leaders to pray. I needed God's Word and encouragement, and in certain moments, I just needed to ignore it all and focus on the things I loved to do.

There are too many families in our communities who are struggling with addictions, depression, and all sorts of abusive behavior. I know that because that was our case. And in the middle of it, prayer was great, but it wasn't enough. It sounds like heresy just writing it, but it's necessary that we talk about it.

I spent eight months with a professional counselor who taught me how to manage my anger, improve my moods, and take ownership of my situation. He gave me books to read, coached me with techniques for relaxation, and he saw Catherine and me together for marriage guidance. He used specific, evidenced-based treatments to treat my conditions and used cognitive behavioral therapy (stuff I would have never considered before), all because after many years in full-time ministry, and after ten years of terrible behavior as a husband, I needed professional help.

I used to be so ashamed to share this, but now I celebrate where God has taken me individually and where He has taken us a couple. And I am so glad I didn't just go down for prayer or a one-time repentance fix, but that I actually invested money and time with a healthcare professional.

It was not perfect. A few times I considered punching my therapist (*Hi Dolan! Love you, Bro*). But after months of weekly sessions, I am absolutely convinced that God took me there.

I have heard stories of people getting healed in one moment. It's happened in my own life in other circumstances, and I pray that for us all, but the reality for most is that the hurts and rejection of the past, combined with actual illness of the mind, require more time, more care, and more attention. It starts with pastors getting help when necessary and it continues with the church as a whole empowering people to do whatever is necessary to be made well. It demands open conversations with those who have overcome, and with those who are still struggling.

It ends with us caring more about people (and their health) than about our limited opinions and hindering theology. The religious mindset wants to control how people heal. It wants to determine the rules of engagement for all scenarios and situations. But spiritual maturity is demonstrated by an increase in realization of the help and grace you need—and the heart of Christ is to heal the brokenhearted.

Maybe you're the brokenhearted in this scenario, if so, *can I encourage you to ask for help?*

And if it takes visiting an actual doctor to help you with your situation, then I know for a fact that Jesus will be holding your hand the whole way through. He did it for me. Jesus is the hope for everyone struggling with mental illness, and the hope for churches that are ignoring it.

It might be a good time to stop pretending and start attending to this real need.

For my sake.

And yours.

Notes

1. Walter Brueggemann, *The Prophetic Imagination* (Minneapolis, MN: Fortress Press, 2001), 88.
2. James Baldwin, *Notes of a Native Son* (Boston: Beacon Press, 1984), 101.
3. Matthew 9:35.
4. Brandon W. Peach, "5 Things Christians Should Know About Depression and Anxiety," *Relevant Magazine*, February 20, 2014, http://archives.relevantmagazine.com/god/church/5-things-christians-should-know-about-depression-and-anxiety. (Accessed March 29, 2017.)

25

WHAT ABOUT JUSTICE?

"To 'do justice' means to render to each what each is due. Justice involves harmony, flourishing, and fairness, and it is based on the image of God in every person—the Imago Dei—that grants all people inalienable dignity and infinite worth."[1]
—Ken Wytsma

Saving the adulterous woman from being brutally killed was an act of justice on the part of Jesus. We know that to the "God-specialists," it would have been lawful to disfigure her to death, but to God, it was ungodly. The woman caught in the act of adultery was the *Imago Dei*, the image of God on earth—created in His likeness, designed for inheritance, and worthy of justice. Just like everyone else.

100% of women of color were created in God's image.

100% of radical Muslims were created in God's image.

100% of undocumented immigrants were created in God's image.

All 100% of you were created as the *Imago Dei*.

The book of the prophet Amos was written while the kingdom of Israel had become a prosperous nation under King Jeroboam II. They were experiencing peace as a nation, great social prestige, and had achieved military might. But the poor suffered like dogs, the foreigners experienced oppression, and the widows and orphans died unattended.

Does that ring any bells? Well, watch out! Here comes the prophet!

I can't stand your religious meetings.

I'm fed up with your conferences and conventions.

I want nothing to do with your religion projects, your pretentious slogans and goals.

I'm sick of your fund-raising schemes, your public relations and image making.

I've had all I can take of your noisy ego-music.

When was the last time you sang to Me?

Do you know what I want?

I want justice—oceans of it.

I want fairness—rivers of it.

That's what I want. That's all I want.

Like alcohol to a wound, the seer spoke the words of God to the people of God, for the sake of God. This passage is Amos 5:21–24, and I'm using *The Message* translation, which reads a lot like Matthew 23. But can you hear the passion in the Father's voice when He asks, *Do you know what I want?* And can you feel the sincerity in His voice when He answers his own questions with the words *justice* and *fairness?*

I do. And I need more of His passion and commitment to it—lots more. You see, most of us can handle *injustice.* We see it on the news, cringe a little, maybe include a prayer and then we let it pass. We're really good at pretending that we care about something that is unfair (and social media has given us a platform to be masters of it). We see racism and we tweet about it. We see war and we comment about it. We see hunger and we share the World Vision website (sometimes without actually signing up for a sponsorship). And I know that social media is a good first step to aware-ness and action, but don't let it deceive you into feeling righteous.

> *That's why God highlights the real problem for us: justice. Justice demands that we do something, and that's precisely what He wants, flowing "like an ever-flowing stream."*[2]

Now, there are two aspects of justice in the Bible that are distinctly defined. The first is called *punitive justice*. It works like this: *an eye for an eye*. What you took from me, I can take from you. It's fair and just enough, and at a core level we all filter life through it. Also, most world govern-ments, employee handbooks, and courses on parenting are ruled by it.

You kill, you get killed.

You rob, you pay back with cash, time, or work.

You are unfaithful to your marriage vows, you lose half of what you own.

This punishment-driven justice creates a sense of fear, of analyzing consequences, and of making decisions based on what will happen to the individual if found guilty. My momma used to call it, *the fear of the Lord*.

But there's another aspect of justice that is at the heart of more than half of the Scripture verses in which the words *righteousness* or *justice* are used. It's precisely what God is talking about in Amos 5. It's called *restor-ative justice*, and this is the kind of fairness that sees all, both the abuser and the abused, as worthy of mercy—as truly *Imago Dei*.

Multiple times a year, I get to witness this in all its splendor. Our church family has connected with a ministry called Proverbs 22:6. Their sole purpose is to bring fathers (who are in prison) together with their children (who are the most likely to go to prison next). In 2016, we had two events inside Central Prison in downtown Raleigh. The first event we did was called, "Forgive Me, Dear." We chaperoned more than fifteen kids into a maximum security facility so that they could spend a day with their fathers. Some of the kids had never even met their fathers before; some had only seen them through a glass and spoken to them through dirty prison phones, and most had never been hugged by their dad.

Volunteers from our church had spent months prior preparing the fathers on how to connect with their little ones. They were teaching them how to ask for forgiveness, how to hold their children's hands, and how to look into their eyes while they spoke to them. There was even some basic training in foot washing.

The reason we brought these kids through five layers of security and inspection was for the deepest moment of reconciliation—and that's precisely what we did. We spent more than six hours creating space so that children between the ages of two and fifteen could be loved by their convicted parent. The prison ward became the temple of the holiest God, and in His presence, rivers of justice flowed.

In the first chapter, I told you about going into prison, preaching the gospel and having an incredible meeting with astonishing fruit. But what Proverbs 22:6 is doing (together with our church family) is producing fruit that will last for generations to come. Children whose parents are in prison are three times more likely to end up in prison themselves. The motivation for these gatherings is to destroy that trend.

Cyril Prabuh, who started and leads Proverbs 22:6, is now funded to give full university scholarships to many of the kids that finish the program. Even the Sketchers shoe company donated thousands of sneakers so that at the end of the first encounter, right after the dad has dried the toes of his darling son or daughter, they got to literally put new shoes on their feet, signifying that they were now heading in a different direction. Proverbs 22:6 is doing this all over the United States and they've been so incredibly successful that prisons where they started in South Carolina are reporting significant reduction of crime and recidivism.

This is restorative justice, where both the oppressor and the oppressed (the father who committed the crime and the innocent children who had nothing to do with it) get to walk in the redemption of Christ. This is the stream that God is thirsty for.

When the Bible talks about justice, I used to imagine a white old man with a long, white beard in a big, white throne, angry and ready to destroy. A Zeus-type figure whose mighty flashes would consume all who broke the law. A perfect Pharisee destroying us with pious rocks.

The magnificent news for you and me, for those kids and those dads, is that the righteous Father is exactly like His humble Son. And if we have seen the Son, then we have seen the Father.

He's the Son who stopped the stoning execution. And He did it because that's what He saw the "white old man on the throne" doing. He did it because the Godhead is more interested in restoring humanity than punishing humans. He did it because the Holy Spirit empowered Him to preach good news to the poor, to heal the brokenhearted, to set at liberty those who are captive, to open the eyes of the blind, and to declare the year of the Lord's favor.

This is His mission statement. Confirmed and approved. Vision casting done!

Jesus, borrowing the words of the prophet Isaiah, clearly articulated His assignment in Luke 4. This was the reason the holy dove descend on Him. It was not to impress us with flashy miracles or uppity sermons. The Holy Spirit came upon the holy Son to empower Him with this holy purpose.

I would like to invite you to make this your own. According to Jesus, *"As the Father has sent me, even so I am sending you."*[3] That means that you have permission, right here, in *Drop the Stones*, to make His mission statement, your own.

Say it out loud, over yourself,

The Spirit of the Lord is upon me, because he has anointed me to proclaim good news to the poor. He has sent me to proclaim liberty to the captives and recovering of sight to the blind, to set at liberty those who are oppressed, to proclaim the year of the Lord's favor.[4]

I agree with Jesus.

And I agree with you.

Notes

1. Ken Wytsma, *Pursuing Justice: The Call to Love and Die for Bigger Things* (Nashville, TN: Thomas Nelson, 2013), 9.
2. Amos 5:24.
3. John 20:21.
4. Luke 4:18–19.

26

PARTY SHEEP

> "The living God is a God of justice and mercy and
> He will be satisfied with nothing less than a people in
> whom his justice and mercy are alive."
> —attributed to Lesslie Newbigin

This chapter might start a bit scary, but I promise you it ends up in a party. Bear with me.

In Matthew 25, Jesus shares one of the most direct revelations of what will happen at the end. He says,

> When the Son of Man comes in his glory, and all the angels with him, he will sit on his glorious throne. All the nations will be gathered before him, and he will separate the people one from another as a shepherd separates the sheep from the goats.[1]

He goes on to explain that the sheep will go to the right and the goats will go to the left; and how that will be determined based on specific action taken with specific people.

I'm not here to argue whether redemption (or at least placement in the kingdom) will be determined by doing any of these actions. *I believe in salvation by faith alone.* But I'm here to remind us of the very distinct summons that Jesus left us sheep.

Then the King will say to those on his right, "Come, you who are blessed by my Father; take your inheritance, the kingdom prepared for you since the creation of the world. For I was hungry and you gave me something to eat, I was thirsty and you gave me something to drink, I was a stranger and you invited me in, I needed clothes and you clothed me, I was sick and you looked after me, I was in prison and you came to visit me."[2]

Very specific.

Food for the hungry.

Water for the thirsty.

Welcoming the stranger.

Clothing the poor.

Caring for the sick.

Visiting the prisoner.

Then the righteous [the ones who manifested justice] *will answer him, "Lord, when did we see you hungry and feed you, or thirsty and give you something to drink? When did we see you a stranger and invite you in, or needing clothes and clothe you? When did we see you sick or in prison and go to visit you?" The King will reply, "Truly I tell you, whatever you did for one of the least of these brothers and sisters of mine, you did for me."[3]*

In the heart of every believer, there is a yearning to worship Jesus. And I know that's the case for you. Well, He made a way for you to touch Him, love Him, dress Him, feed Him, visit Him, care for Him, and minister to Him on a daily basis.

And as David Ruis likes to say, "The fragrance of worship is justice."[4]

One of the definitions for the word *worship* in the New Testament is *to get close enough to kiss.* And we truly can be that close to Jesus when we attend to the least. What we do for them, we do for Him.

Literally, not figuratively.

Now, because of the compassion Jesus manifested to the disenfranchised, because of the simplicity of His message and the fact that you could leave his three-day conference with a basket full of bread and fish, the majority of the demographic that followed Jesus were the poor and needy.

The New Testament makes note of those who were rich like the Pharisees, who provided a grave, or the wealthy women who gave finances for His ministry, not because they were more important, but because they were the minority.

This continued to be the case in the book of Acts. Peter declared in his first miracle, "*Silver or gold I do not have, but what I do have I give you. In the name of Jesus Christ of Nazareth, walk.*"[5] That was the style—give what you have. So the widows were taken care of, the orphans found a home, the sick were healed by shadows, and nobody went hungry.

When Paul was about to start his world-shaking ministry, his leaders gave him a straightforward encouragement. It was not to preach biblically or start successful churches. Above everything else they asked him to *remember the poor*. And Paul replied, saying, "*The very thing I was eager to do.*"[6]

Then James, the son of Mary and the half-brother of Jesus, wrote what is considered to be the first book of New Testament. It's an exhortation to the Jewish church, which James was the lead pastor of. In it he says,

> *Suppose a brother or sister is without clothes and daily food. If one of you says to them, "Go in peace; keep warm and well fed," but does nothing about their physical needs, what good is it? In the same way, faith by itself, if it is not accompanied by action, is dead.*[7]

Dead!

From the early days of Christianity there was already a separation between the impoverished and the wealthy that needed to be corrected. Note that this letter was written to Christians who were dispersed because of persecution. James is not even writing to people who are in a comfortable living situation. Still, the bold preacher speaks strongly against favoritism (calling it a sin) and encourages the church to care for the poor.

Because you know, *faith without action is dead!*

Again, our salvation is not dependent on our works. On the final moment of a whole life dedicated to sin and selfishness, a man can find redemption and sit with you and me at the banqueting table forever.

Nevertheless, and I know you can agree with me, on the days we share the gospel, the times we give extravagantly to the poor, when we manifest the justice of God, when we stand up for the weak—those are the days we go to bed feeling most alive.

There, we enjoy the pleasure of God. The same daily pleasure the Son felt while being obedient to the Father (and being surrounded by the disenfranchised). I believe it is possible to follow Jesus for our own sakes but not for others. Ours souls might be saved, but our lives will be wasted. And what a sad waste that would be.

Loving and living justice is quite possibly the most exhilarating thing there is. It's an adventure beyond compare—and God is inviting us to the hard work of great jubilee!

Remember how I told you about the "Forgive me, Dear" event? Well, on our second visit to the prison with Proverbs 22:6, the event was called "Celebrate." It was around the holiday season, so the prison staff had a Christmas tree up and there were guards who happily joined us even though it was their day off. The first event had been so successful that we added extra children and dads to this next one.

And it was a party of epic proportions.

I'm not even trying to be cute; it was probably the best gathering I attended all year long. We started with tons of games. We then moved to a talent show that the kids had prepared for their parents. There was rap, hip-hop, Drake-like dancing, hilarious comedians (aka me), and a plethora of sweet performances. After that, we had a special dance between the dads and their daughters. We played the classic song "You Are So Beautiful" and watched as these hard men melted while slow dancing with their baby girls. They took time to speak life and identity over them, and they sang the song over and over again.

Our cheeks were drenched in tears but our hearts overflowed with delight.

We then served a delicious lunch of pulled pork, fried chicken, coleslaw, hush puppies, salads, sweet tea, desserts, and more. The atmosphere in the room was so full of happiness and peace that the guards and the warden sat down to eat their meals at the same time that the dads and kids ate together at nicely decorated tables, while no one guarded the doors.

Of course, we danced some more. We played the classic Kool & the Gang song "Celebration," and we actually kept singing and moving through the soul train, even after the song had ended. *Celebrate good times…come on!*

You have to visualize these dads and their kids in the middle of a maximum security ward having the best Christmas of their lives. There were candy canes, carol singing, more games, more dancing, the gospel being preached, and the kingdom of God manifesting. We finished the day by leading the men in a Father's blessing over their sons and daughters. And it was my most-fun day of 2016.

My faith was alive that day. As the master of ceremonies and the preacher of the five-minute sermon, there was nothing better for me to do than to be there. And I did the least of all. "Celebrate" happened because of the combined herculean effort of the prisoners, volunteers, paid staff, correctional employees, and the Lord who works justice.

Cue Luke 14:12–14:

When you give a dinner or a banquet, do not invite your friends or your brothers or your relatives or rich neighbors, lest they also invite you in return and you be repaid. But when you give a feast, invite the poor, the crippled, the lame, the blind, and you will be blessed, because they cannot repay you. For you will be repaid at the resurrection of the just.

Maybe if we tried doing what Jesus said, we could see what Jesus meant. So where are the prostitutes and drug addicts in your city? What's the name of your town's correctional facility? Who are the hungry and the broken in your community?

Find them quick.

Jesus is waiting for you there.

Ready to party, and close enough to kiss.

Notes

1. Matthew 25:31–32 NIV.
2. Verses 34–36 NIV.
3. Matthew 25:37–40 NIV.
4. David Ruis, *The Justice God Is Seeking* (Bloomington, MN: Bethany House, 2006), 18.
5. Acts 3:6 NIV.
6. Galatians 2:10.
7. James 2:15–17 NIV.

ACT 3

THE GOD

He could feel the freshness of the morning in his nostrils. The air he breathed in was the air he had called into being, yet he still was in awe of the feeling in his lungs. With hope he scanned the colors of the sunrise and then closed his eyes. But in that fleeting moment he remembered the words of the crowd, "You have a demon!" Once again, Jesus felt tempted to leave Jerusalem. The religious leaders in the city were persistent with their disapproval and they watched his every move, looking for an opportunity to rush the inevitable.

"Do unto others as you want them to do to you," the Rabbi muttered under his breath, and smiled again. He could sense the Father in Jerusalem, and he only did what he saw the Father doing. "I'm here, Abba. Let Your will be done."

He walked down the winding path from the Mount of Olives and arrived at the temple. The early risers quickly gathered around him. They pushed to sit close to his feet so he made a point to look every single one of them in the eye at least once during his twenty-minute sermon.

All of a sudden the smiles of the people turned into horror as a mob of figures dressed in black pushed through the crowd. A cloud of dust billowed up as everyone in attendance quickly rose to their feet and moved out of the way. Standing in the middle was a short Pharisee shaking with anger, quoting the law and barely blinking.

"*What do you say we do?*"

With one hand the man was squeezing a rock and with the other he was squeezing the wrist of a half-naked lady. Then, with all of his strength, he dragged her closer to the middle, exposing her to the crowd, to the men, and to Christ.

Jesus took a deep breath, looking for the hope he had found in the sunset, but his lungs filled with dust. He could sense the fear that gripped the woman, the disgust traveling through the crowd, the rage that filled the legalists, and a compassion that moved him to the ground.

Oh yes, he remembered being this close to the dirt before. He remembered the innocence of the first ones created. And he remembered the love that drove him from the throne.

The Messiah began to push his fingers through the dirt, peering into the soul of everyone in the crowd. The men got antsy, more demanding; their howls were almost deafening. After a few minutes, the hubbub dissipated and Jesus found himself kneeling before a condemned woman and being reminded what the law of Moses said.

"Rabbi," said the short angry man again, "this woman has been caught in the act of adultery. And you know that the Law of Moses commands us to stone such women. So what do you say we do?"

Jesus whispered to himself again, "I was not sent into the world to condemn the world, but in order that the world might be saved through me."

"Saved."

"Through."

"Me."

In that moment, God stood up, and said to all who remained, "*Let him who is without sin, be the first to throw a stone at her.*"

The men were stunned, baffled, and defeated. Their heads went low and their eyes noticed the words Jesus had written on the ground. Caiaphas was the first to drop the stone in his hand and walk away. And as a growing rhythm, the silence that had gripped the moment turned into a glorious sound of praise as every rock and stone hit the dirt. The Pharisees, scribes, and teachers of the Law left the temple of the holy God, saved from themselves.

Jesus had bent down once again to write some more and it wasn't until he was alone with the woman that he picked himself up and asked, "Woman, where are they? Does no one condemn you?"

She stood in front of him clothed with relief and dressed in salvation. He could tell by the way she was looking at him that she had found her true love.

"No one, Lord," she replied, squeezing her watery eyes shut. "No one."

The God, the Lord, the Savior, then said, "Neither do I condemn you. Go, and sin no more."

27

BACK TO THE OBVIOUS

"This is what God's kingdom is like: a bunch of outcasts and oddballs gathered at a table, not because they are rich or worthy or good, but because they are hungry, because they said yes. And there's always room for more."[1]
—*Rachel Held Evans*

Here's a bit of foundational Christianity:

Love the hurting.

Feed the hungry.

Preach resurrection.

Repeat with joy (even in suffering).

I feel confident in calling it *foundational* because it was delivered by the incarnate Word of God, and He did it full of grace and truth.

Brian McLaren may have expressed it best when he wrote,

The more one respects Jesus, the more one must be brokenhearted, embarrassed, furious, or some combination thereof when one considers what we Christians have done with Jesus. That's certainly true when it comes to calling Jesus Lord, something we Christians do a lot, often without the foggiest idea of what we mean. Has he become (I shudder to ask this) less our Lord and more our Mascot?[2]

I shudder to ask this myself.

For some reason, the simple gospel has been convoluted into something else. It has been prostituted for personal gain, distorted by irrational politics, and mutated for profit and glory. In turn, it has become something so conflicting that it actually works against the very message it's trying to proclaim.

Do you remember the telephone game? The one where you start with a one-line whisper like, "Jimmy likes Abby." Then, that information is shared exclusively with the person to the right, and from one curious ear to the next, the private news begins to acquire adjectives? "Jimmy really likes Abby" goes to the next person who adds, "Jimmy loves Abby like crazy!" Unto the next, "Jimmy and Abby are in love"…and on and on it goes.

When the last person shares the first whisper out loud, the original "Jimmy likes Abby" ends up sounding like, "Jimmy got Abby pregnant outside of marriage and for some reason they both hate chocolate."

Well, Christianity is kind of like that.

We have been whispering our versions of the good news. We have different churches, in different nations, forming different denominations, and sharing *their* version of the gospel. Before long, the good news became bad.

But thank God for Matthew, Mark, Luke, and John! We get to go back and regain the original information. We have official (heaven sent) confirmation of the message; the news cannot be lost in translation. And the Bible is as clear as water: God is love. Jesus is the Savior. The Holy Spirit will remind us. Basically, "The Trinity likes Jimmy and Abby and Carlos."

There is no interpretation required. No need for theological debates. This message is simple; it's been confirmed and validated, *"For God so loved the world…."*[3]

Unfortunately, we want to stick to the version we've created.

Throughout the centuries, religious men have adjusted the story to accommodate their narrative. So the Bible message, and most particularly, the gospel message, has been whispered throughout history, and the message we hear now, does not sound much like the message that was first shared two thousand years ago in Capernaum and Jerusalem. The message of love, grace, and mercy has been tragically transformed into a message of law, judgment, and misery.

I have heard Bill Johnson say that "God never violates His Word, but He's quite comfortable violating our understanding of His Word." I love that because therein lies the problem: our interpretation of the Word, the lens through which we look at Scripture. Let's start then with a simple statement, a statement that will anchor this exchange: *Jesus Christ is perfect theology.*

Let me confirm it with these words spoken by Jesus Himself:

"Whoever has seen me has seen the Father."[4]

"No one has ever seen God, but the one and only Son, who is himself God and is in closest relationship with the Father."[5]

Or as Jesus brilliantly said, *"The Scriptures point to me!"*[6]

I think that most of us agree with this concept. We accept the truth of who Jesus is as the Son of God, but we disagree with the radical things He said (and the scandalous things He did). In some shape or form we all have modified His persona to accommodate our current view of Him, instead of allowing His presence and His person to modify our current view of everything else.

We use His name, but we ignore His ways. Our intentions are good but our doctrine is cruel. However, Jesus is too perfect, too real, and too God for us not to humble ourselves and allow Him to change our hearts and minds. He is perfect theology and the whole point of the story! *Even the story itself.*

The Son of God is the good news, delivering good news, mostly for bad people. So if you think you're one of the good people, then you'll miss it completely.

Now, according to Jesus, there are ways for us to currently have access to His very Person. There are multiple spiritual revelations of our place in Him, our unity with Him, and His union with us. Yet, for example, in the story of Robert and Catherine in chapter 4, Jesus is both Robert and Catherine. He is the hungry one being fed, and He is the lovely one feeding.

He has made Himself fully available to us, in each other. Of course, that does not take away from the fact that He is ruling and reigning as the King of Kings and the Lord of Lords at the right hand of the Father. It just means that He's available right here, also. We can touch Him, see Him, experience Him, and even smell Him.

Sometimes He looks like Catherine.

And sometimes He smells like Robert.

But He never acts like the selfish-religious me.

"Go and learn what this means," Jesus said. *"'I desire mercy, and not sacrifice.' For I came not to call not the righteous, but sinners."*[7]

I agree with the daring words of Dallas Willard:

> The greatest issue facing the world today, with all its heartbreaking needs, is whether those who, by profession or culture, are identified as "Christians" will become disciples—students, apprentices, practitioners—of Jesus Christ, steadily learning from him how to live the life of the Kingdom of the Heavens into every corner of human existence.[8]

Notes

1. Rachel Held Evans, *Searching for Sunday: Loving, Leaving, and Finding the Church* (Nashville: Thomas Nelson, 2015), 148.
2. Brian D. McLaren, *A Generous Orthodoxy* (Grand Rapids, MI: Zondervan, 2006), 80.
3. John 3:16.
4. John 14:9.
5. John 1:18 NIV.
6. John 5:39 TLB.
7. Matthew 9:13.
8. Dallas Willard, *The Great Omission: Reclaiming Jesus's Essential Teachings on Discipleship* (New York: HarperOne, 2014), xv.

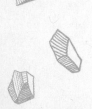

28

THE FLESH

"God is like Jesus. God has always been like Jesus. There has
never been a time when God was not like Jesus. We have not
always known what God is like—but now we do."[1]
—*Brian Zahnd*

Yes, Brian, now we do. Now we know that the supernatural, everlasting,
Creator of all is the human Jesus.

Jesus *is* God. And any "god" idea-suspicion-version-image that is not
exactly like Jesus is not God at all. The problem with that is that Jesus
looks like a man—a humble, kind, tender, willing-to-die-for-scumbags
kind of a man.

And we thought God would be more powerful, more dominant, and
hungrier to prove Himself. But then Jesus came and He was more concerned with healing the sick, feeding the poor, and befriending the worst.

We thought lepers were being punished by God under the curse of the
sovereign Lord, but God came around and touched them, healed them,
loved them, and turned them into evangelists.

We thought celebrities and politicians were the right people for God to
use, but God showed up and chose fishermen, tax collectors, and prostitutes.
He trained them, believed in them, and showed them a superior kingdom.

We thought that God was angry and disappointed with humanity, but God made Himself human; He lived a human life, died a human death, and kept His human body.

Incarnation.

God showed up and forgave the sins that shouldn't be forgiven. He loved the unlovable just as much as He loved children. Instead of destroying the Romans, He ended up healing their servants. He denied the temptation to use political power to change the world. Instead of being the God we wanted Him to be, He was less religious, less of a war monger, less sectarian, and less like me. Instead of killing His enemies, He died to make them friends.

Jürgen Moltmann wrote, "When the crucified Jesus is called 'the image of the invisible God', the meaning is that *this* is God, and God is like *this*."[2]

In the famous opening to his Gospel, the apostle John wrote, *"And the Word became flesh, and dwelt among us, and we beheld His glory, the glory as of the only begotten from the Father, full of grace and truth."*[3]

The Word of God, who is brimming with sweetness and veracity, came to tabernacle among us, and while with us, manifested in life what was spoken only in Spirit.

Now it's our turn.

It's time for *our* theology, *our* creeds, and *our* beliefs, to get some flesh on them.

Full of grace and truth.

Notes

1. Brian Zahnd, "God Is Like Jesus," *Brian Zahnd* (blog), August 11, 2011, https://brianzahnd.com/2011/08/god-is-like-jesus-2/. (Accessed March 26, 2017.)
2. Jürgen Moltmann, *The Crucified God: The Cross of Christ as the Foundation and Criticism of Christian Theology* (Minneapolis: Fortress Publishers, 1993), 205.
3. John 1:14 NKJV.

29

THE FLESH TOO

*"Once the Word has become flesh, all the books in the
world can't do justice to it. Only flesh can: your flesh, my flesh."*[1]
—N. T. Wright

One time I was on a mission trip in Costa Rica and we were paying prostitutes their hourly rate so that they would instead come to hear about God's love for them. We welcomed them into a safe house, fed them a delicious meal, and encouraged them with Scripture verses and inspired prayers.

I thought it was terrible idea and a contamination of mission funds. I also thought it would set the wrong precedent and that people would always expect to be paid in order to attend this kind of a service. Finally, I thought that the boys on my team would be too tempted by the ladies of the night (and I thought this because *I* was afraid of being too tempted by the ladies of the night).

This seems to be my life story, everyone. It all goes well when I agree with God, but it's life-changing when I don't…and this might be due to the fact that He loves me as I am, but He loves me too much to leave me as I am.

You've been warned.

After discussing the options for the afternoon, the leader of the ministry took us to pray for the pimp who controlled the area. He actually had a throne built in the middle of an interior garden in the center of San Jose. Men and women, half of them boys and girls, who were employed by him had to sit at his feet. He did not want prayer for himself, but he led us to one of his sick workers who was lying on a bed with a massive open wound caused by an untreated case of HIV/AIDS. I remember entering the room, taking a deep breath, and crying uncontrollably. Then, two guys from our team picked up the young prostitute and carried him two blocks to an urgent care center. We paid good money so they would take him in, and I knew then and there that investing in these people was money (and time) well spent.

We went back to the brothel and asked for permission from the pimp to pay his employees to come to a small, second-story room where they could hear the voice of God and eat a good meal. He agreed, and off we went.

I was nineteen years old at the time, leading a team of students from the School of Ministry in Toronto, Canada. Together with other young people like myself, we spent a whole afternoon taking our eyes off of the hot pants and the exposed cleavages and trying to love each man and woman as Christ loves the church. We saw many tears, many prayers of repentance, and many people connecting with the local church leaders.

Yes, that afternoon changed my perspective, but I wish we could have done more (and we should have done more). The ministry of Jesus was not just about a moment of healing but a deconstruction of the systems that cause the sickness. I've spent most of my Christian life just trying to get people to become Christians. All I wanted was for them to *not* go to hell when they died, yet all the while I was willing to accept the hell on earth they were experiencing while alive.

The flesh of God came to destroy the works of the devil; the body of Christ is meant to do the same. We need salvation, of course, but we are saved *into* His kingdom as much as we are saved *from* the kingdom of darkness. And the kingdom of God is righteousness, peace, and joy in the Holy Spirit—not just for Carlos but also for everyone else.

I could never see this before. I wanted Jesus to save *me* but judge *them*. I wanted Him to have compassion when it came to my sin but I wanted him to "teach them a lesson" when it came to theirs. Everyone that I liked deserved the God of the New Testament, but everyone that I disliked deserved the God of the Old Testament.

Seriously, in the deepest part of me, I think that I still want God to hate the people I hate. I want Him to be okay with the wrongdoings I don't consider a big deal. I want God to vote like me, sound like me, and go to the same church I go to. And I want God to be more Latino.

But when I discover (over and over again) that God is like Jesus, and that He is still doing "Jesus things," I enter into the delight available for those who claim Jesus as their King.

N. T. Wright also explained it like this:

This is the really scary thing...not that Jesus might be identified with a remote, lofty, imaginary being, but that God, the real God, the one true God, might actually look like Jesus...a shrewd Palestinian Jewish villager who drank wine with His friends, agonized over the plight of His people, taught in strange stories and pungent aphorisms, and was executed by the occupying forces.... To say that Jesus is in some sense God is of course to make a startling statement about Jesus. It is also to make a stupendous claim about God.[2]

Of course, there are a lot of things I love about God the Son. But there are also a lot of things I find very difficult to embrace—turn the other cheek, forgive seventy times seven times, wash people's feet, raise the dead, and so on. They are not difficult to embrace because I don't believe in them (I kind of have to because I'm a pastor and God said them). It's more that I am terrible at them. I am naturally better suited for Pharisaism, i.e. read the Bible, interpret it to my liking, judge those that disagree with me, and stay away from my enemies.

Yes, I have a problem with this version of God that loves so well, forgives so hard, and wants everyone to be saved.[3] But Jesus is the only legitimate version there is. So what I truly have a problem is with *me*.

God will not change.

I guess I'll have to.

I guess, *we'll* have to.

Notes

1. N. T. Wright, *John for Everyone, Part 2: Chapters 11–21* (Louisville: Westminster John Knox Press, 2004), 170.
2. N. T. Wright, *Who Was Jesus?* (Grand Rapids, MI: Wm. B. Eerdmans Publishing Co., 2014), 52.
3. See 1 Timothy 2:4.

30

TELENOVELA

*"Be like Jesus: Spend enough time with sinners to ruin your repu-
tation with religious people."* [1]
—Joshua Harris

When the Pharisees called Jesus "a friend of sinners" they were trying to insult Him. They were also trying to drive home this point: "He's enjoying himself in their company!"

Or as Jesus explained it Himself, *"The Son of Man came eating and drinking, and they say, 'Here is a glutton and a drunkard, a friend of tax collectors and sinners.' But wisdom is proved right by her deeds."* [2]

The teachers of the law wanted the people of the land to understand that Jesus wasn't in proximity with sinners because He had a hidden (religious) agenda. It's not like He was a covert agent, pretending to be something that He was not, so that He could fulfill a holier purpose.

He really was their friend.

He ate with the scum, drank wine from their same cup, laughed and cried, argued and hugged, and spoke theology and politics together, as only real friends could, and the saintly superiors hated His guts for it.

You see, neediness gives us the opening to become a solution, but friendship is how we earn the right to be heard. The people came to Jesus because

He could heal them; He met their needs. But those same people listened to Jesus because He befriended them, and they became His sidekicks.

The most satisfying way to reach people with the God-story is when they also have permission to reach us with their stories. I learned this from a man who is in love with the worst people. His name is Chris Hoke, and as a chaplain in maximum-security prisons, he discovered that the best place of connection was when he started to share his struggles with the inmates who were struggling the most. His candor and non-pretentiousness allowed him to win the hearts of the toughest men.

After a reading of his book, *Wanted*, he told me over a beer, "Just ask them to pray for you, Carlos." Such a simple suggestion, yet such a powerful revelation.

So I gave it a go, and I've never looked back.

Every time I visit my friends in the inner city or preach inside of prisons, I ask them for prayer. It disarms the lie that says that I am somehow superior, holier, or more connected with heaven.

Jesus did the same with His closest friends. He made the guys who sucked at praying His primary intersession team. It's best exemplified on the night before He was about to be crucified. He went up to the garden of Gethsemane (the place where the olive oil was pressed) and in the squeeze of the weighty night, Jesus got real with His words. *"'My soul is overwhelmed with sorrow to the point of death,' he said to them. 'Stay here and keep watch.'"*[3]

Like a *telenovela* with tense language and melodramatic expressions, the perfect Messiah revealed His humanity to the most basic level.

"I feel like dying, because I feel finished."

"My heart is aching, I need my friends."

He goes a bit further from them and begins to pray to Abba Father. He does not pretend to be anything but a man who needs His buddies, and a son who needs His daddy. Almost fainting, He prays, *"Abba, Father, all things are possible for you. Remove this cup from me. Yet not what I will, but what you will."*[4] As if to say, "I embrace what you have for me, even if my human will prefers the opposite."

No wonder Jesus needed His friends to watch with Him. He was tempted more than ever. He could literally feel the lure of sin crouching at the door. And He could've made the choice to disobey the Father: His will could have been in contradiction (which caused Him to sweat blood, feel the gloom, and collapse on the floor).

He went back to His friends after barely enduring the torment, and they were all asleep. He asked them, disappointedly, *"Could you not watch with me one hour?"*[5]

I told you.

Telenovela.

Go read it in Mark 14. Honestly, put this book down and go experience the humanity of God, fully expressed in the Son, Jesus.

It's so beautiful, because He's just like us: tired, exasperated, frustrated with His friends, and in a battle with His flesh—and yet without sin.

The disciples (bless them) had no clue about the magnitude of this moment. To them it was just another day with the cursing-fig-trees-when-He's-hungry teacher-prophet. Yet Jesus, even though He knew their frailty and their upcoming betrayal, still asked for His friends to watch and wait with Him. He knew that exposing them to His moment of weaknesses would not make them less strong; quite the opposite, actually. To see the God-Human endure such "ungodly" emotions gave them permission to be fully human themselves. And that's the kind of friend we want to have (and be)—not pretenders, but open books to the human experience.

An experience that is incomplete without the need for Abba.

And a few crappy friends.

Father Gregory Boyle wrote in his wonderful book *Tattoos on the Heart*,

> You stand with the least likely to succeed until success is succeeded by something more valuable: kinship. You stand with the belligerent, the surly, and the badly behaved until bad behavior is recognized for the language it is: the vocabulary of the deeply wounded and of those whose burdens are more than they can bear.[6]

Our generation is starving for friendship. Social media is sending us this message loud and clear. We are all desperate for connection, but the church keeps producing more and more plastic meetings, sermons, and associations. We keep trying so hard to have the perfect song, with the perfect theology, with the perfect sound, and the perfect timing. We get preoccupied with big buildings and comfortable meetings while people are hurting, lonely, and desperate for meaning.

What if you took the "friend of sinners approach"? Bring wine to their parties, put a hand on their leprosy, invite them to your intimate struggles, and then give your life for their benefit.

This is the way that God understands friendship—to be so connected to their journey that you absorb their disdain; to be confused as gluttons and drunkards because the people you love and befriend are gluttons and drunkards themselves.

And it is legitimate to ask yourself, *If I'm not reaching the same people Christ reached, am I even preaching the same gospel Jesus preached?*

Notes

1. Joshua Harris, Twitter post, June 1, 2015, 7:02 p.m., http://twitter.com/HarrisJosh.
2. Matthew 11:19 NIV.
3. Mark 14:34 NIV.
4. Mark 14:36.
5. Matthew 26:40.
6. Gregory Boyle, *Tattoos on the Heart* (New York: Free Press, 2010), 179.

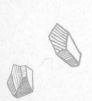

31

WHO'S THE MAIN CHARACTER?

"If you're using the Bible to argue for oppression,
exclusion, or violence, then you've misunderstood both
the story and the storyteller."[1]
—*Nathan Hamm*

The main question we need to be asking is not "Who is God sending to hell?" Instead, it is "What did God do when He came to earth?" The most important question is not even "Does Jesus hate sin?" but rather, "How would Jesus love this sinner?"

If we keep trying to make the Bible about the four verses we use to judge a certain person, or the five verses that guide our selective morality, then we will miss the main character of the story: the Lord Himself.

Rapture. Conservative. Trinity. Masturbation. Revival. These are just a few of the many words that are not found in the Bible. And if you disregard words that are articles, conjunctions, prepositions, and such, the most common word found in Scripture is *Lord.* It occurs 6,782 times between Genesis and Revelation.

The next twenty-nine words that appear most in the Bible are…

God–4,293   Israel–2,509

Man–2,747   People–2,271

King–2,124

Jesus–953

Son–1,980

Father–944

Men–1,860

Name–934

House–1,840

Heart–925

Day–1,759

Days–923

Children–1,727

David–881

Land–1,641

Moses–804

Things–1,438

Place–798

Hand–1,419

Time–787

Earth–1,088

Judah–756

Sons–1,061

Word–737

Jerusalem–956

Evil–657

City–953

Notice that in the top thirty words in the Bible, the first word with a purely negative connotation is *Evil*.

At number thirty.

Yes, some of the top twenty-nine were used as negative in different scenarios, but the point is that the Bible prioritizes words like *good, heart, Father, children, Jesus,* and *people,* above words like *death, sword, enemies, and judgment*—words that don't even make it to the top fifty.

This is not about watering down the Scriptures, this is about prioritizing what the Scriptures prioritize. And I know this is a simplistic view of the complexity and intricacies of the Bible, but maybe simple is what we need. Like children learning to read, the more you see one word, the quicker it is to learn it and become fluent with it.

Sadly, we recognize the negative words more than the positive ones. They are highlighted above the rest. Our human brains, scientifically proven to become more attached to the negative than the positive, have been deceived to believe that the Bible story is more about *immortality* and *war* than about *beauty* and *rest.* But even when we isolate every single negative word in the Bible, if we are looking at Scripture through the lens of

Jesus (which is the only legitimate way to look at it) then *sin* and *death* and *hell* and *Satan* will be filtered through the *cross*, the *love*, and the *forgiveness* of *Christ*.

The book that starts with God, prioritizes *Adonai*, and tells us what *Yahweh* likes and dislikes…reveals who *I AM* truly is. And He is love.

The compartmentalization of the Bible has allowed us to pick and choose the verses we want to highlight, and often we highlight them out of context. Since it's possible to go from chapter-whatever to verse-whatever, we forget that each word was written as a brushstroke in a masterpiece. Most of the Good Book was not written to be read piece by piece, but as the ultimate script leading us to the ultimate name: *the Lord Himself.* It's the narrative that brings us to Christ; the story of God's grace; a collection of poems and history, written by imperfect humans inspired by the Spirit of truth.

My young children are already starting to understand the main theme of the Bible: *the Lord is the protagonist and He is amazing.* (And this is based on the iPad version of the Bible for kids that we read together after watching *Inside Out* for the fiftieth hundred millionth time.)

The Lord's name *is* everywhere. It's found 6,782 times between Genesis and Revelation. As Brian Zahnd says, "What the Bible does infallibly is point us to Jesus Christ."[2] And remember that stoning the woman who was caught in the act of adultery was biblical, but it was not Christ-like.

Whatever *the Lord* says, goes.

Notes

1. Nathan Hamm, Twitter post, August 11, 2011, 9:37 a.m., http://twitter.com/NathanHamm.
2. Brian Zahnd, "Scripture as Witness to the Word of God," BrianZahnd.com (blog), January 1, 2014, https://brianzahnd.com/2014/01/scripture-witness-word-god/. (Accessed March 25, 2017.)

32

THE TITLE, SERVANT

"Sometimes the best evangelism is telling people you're a
Christian and not being a jerk."[1]
—*John Pavlovitz*

What if Christians were known more for our *feet washing* than our *sin bashing*? What if kindness was the main tool we used to demonstrate God's kingdom? What if instead of trying to lead the world, we would instead focus on serving it?

I have based most of my understanding of leadership and influence on the premise that God wants me to be a leader and an influencer. Yet the more I get into the story of Jesus (His words, His actions, and His life) the more I realize that God has no interest in me being a leader. He wants me to be a servant, and that puts me in a bind.

Because while I like the title *servant*, I just don't like being treated like one.

Of course I have intentionally chosen positions of leadership in my life. They make me feel valuable and significant.

Pastor.

Chief Editor.

Creative Director.

Husband.

Dad.

And to every one of those titles (whether I say it or not) I attach a sense of leadership (and rule) to them—at least more than I attach a sense of servanthood.

The King of Kings, on the other hand, said,

You call me Teacher and Lord, and you are right, for so I am. If I then, your Lord and Teacher, have washed your feet, you also ought to wash one another's feet. For I have given you an example, that you also should do just as I have done to you.[2]

Faced with this, I honestly have to ask myself, when was the last time I actually washed feet? Literally, not figuratively?

Heck, when was the last time I even figuratively washed someone's feet?

Recently, I was asking God in prayer to open doors for ministry. I wanted more opportunities to preach in prisons, foreign nations, big stages, or small gatherings (you know, because I'm so humble and cool).

The Father answered my request with His own question: *"Who are you going to serve when you go there?"*

I answered, "Duh! I want to serve those prisoners, the crowds, and Your people."

His gentle reply, "Do you really want to be there for them, or for how it looks on social media when you visit prisoners? When you're on the big stage, are you there for their sakes, or for *the money shot* picture?"

My answer,

...

...

...

People have told me that I have a "leadership calling" on my life. But now I'm concerned, because not once did they say that because I was washing someone's feet, which is the physical expression of godly leadership. Just as the bread and the wine are a physical manifestation of a spiritual truth, so is feet washing a down-to-earth revelation of a heavenly reality.

So I'm here to say, I got it all wrong.

Again.

(Lord, have mercy!)

Let's take a five-second interlude. It would be tempting to start thinking of past leaders, teachers, pastors, and bosses while writing about servanthood. But I am not writing so you can get angry/cynical, about/toward them. This is an encouragement for you and me. However, if you have endured legitimate control/manipulation, then this becomes an invitation to forgive their mountaintop ways so that we can move in grace, with Christ, in the opposite direction.

Deal?

Now, let me give you an even stronger text to support the outrageous claim that Jesus is somehow *anti-leadership.*

I'll remind you of Matthew 23:8–12.

And once again this is the Lord of Lords speaking.

But you are not to be called rabbi, for you have one teacher, and you are all brothers. And call no man your father on earth, for you have one Father, who is in heaven. Neither be called instructors, for you have one instructor, the Christ. The greatest among you shall be your servant. Whoever exalts himself will be humbled, and whoever humbles himself will be exalted.

What are we doing?

And this is an honest (loaded) question.

Why are we teaching people so much about leadership and influence? How come we spend so much money on books, seminars, and conferences to be better at it? Obviously, leadership is important. It is a New Testament concept with incredible examples like Mary Magdalene, Junia, James, and Paul. But the Word of God in the flesh, Jesus Christ Himself, never used the word *leadership.*

Not once.

His continual invitation was for those who wanted leadership to recognize that the way up is down, that the way forward is back, and that the kingdom of God is only found when we are not building our own kingdoms. This is all proven by the fact that every time His own disciples talked about thrones and position, Jesus redirected those desires toward feet, dirt, brokenness, and sacrificial love.

And Jesus leads us by example in this. He resisted the temptation of the enemy to rule the nations though force. He resisted the invitation of the crowds to be an earthly king. Jesus didn't use His authority to build an empire. He did not use His power to make people bow before Him. He didn't force people to serve Him—He served them!

The perfect Son of God fixed broken chairs, washed feet, died on a cross, and cooked breakfast for His friends.

Here we are again, dear church.

Standing on top of the mountain.

Wanting power, influence, and control.

But Jesus said *no* to that temptation…and He invites us to do the same, *"For even the Son of Man came **not** to be served but to serve, and to give his life as a ransom for many."*[3]

Maybe it will help us to see what leadership titles in the original language meant; as used in the New Testament:

1. "Bishops" are guardians (*episkopos*).

2. "Pastors" are caretakers (*poimén*).

3. "Ministers" are table-waiters (*diakonos*).

4. "Elders" are wise old men (*presbuteros*).

5. "Apostles" are sent ones (*apóstolos*).

6. "Deacons" are waiters (*diakonos*).

The extraordinary leader Paul wrote to the church in Philippi: *"Do nothing from selfish ambition or conceit, but in humility count others more significant than yourselves."*[4]

If we are going to talk about leadership, let's make sure it's in the arrow model and not the pyramid. I learned this comparison from Duncan Smith (a leader I love and gladly serve). Picture a pyramid bowing down to Jesus. At His feet it becomes the head of an arrow. It goes from being this: △ to being this: ▷.

Pyramids are found in deserts; they are full of dead men's bones; they are a relic of the past; and they don't go anywhere.

Arrows come in groups; they are used as weapons; they move forward; and they are launched by someone.

A true (Jesus-like) leader is one that goes ahead (launched by Jesus Himself) not one who stands on top (overpowering the rest). I would like to be an arrow in all my areas of influence, that way I can destroy the pyramid model of leadership and become one who is sent ahead—launched by God into the forefront of the battlefield; to serve, to love, and to die for my friends.

It starts by washing dishes at home and serving meals at your local soup kitchen. It continues with preparing amazing sermons for the church and then spending quality time with people after you leave the stage. It can grow into the daily habit of manifesting consideration in your work place, getting people coffee, opening the door for your coworkers, and going the extra mile for your enemies.

Serving those who "should be serving you" is quite possibly the most authentic pronouncement of Christianity there is. It puts flesh to the Christ who came down from His throne to be a servant of all. And this Christ is still saying,

> *You know that those who are considered rulers of the Gentiles lord it over them, and their great ones exercise authority over them.* ***But it shall not be so among you.*** *But whoever would be great among you must be your servant, and whoever would be first among you must be slave of all.*[5]

We agree with you Lord.

It shall not be so.

Notes

1. John Pavlovitz, Twitter post, October 29, 2015, 9:05 a.m., http://twitter.com/johnpavlovitz.
2. John 13:13–15.
3. Mark 10:45.
4. Philippians 2:3.
5. Mark 10:42–45.

33

YOU LACK ONE THING

"Giving is true having."[1]
—*Charles Spurgeon*

A few years ago the private jet of a famous prosperity gospel preacher ran off a runway. Fortunately, nobody was seriously hurt, except the old jet. So the preacher launched a fundraising campaign to get his followers to pay approximately sixty-five million dollars for a new Gulfstream G650. He suggested to his listeners that they all commit to giving "three hundred dollars or more." The jet he wanted was the fastest plane ever built in civilian aviation. But after receiving immediate and intense backlash, the preacher ended the fundraising.

Sadly, the church as a whole looked like a greedy machine. *Again.*

At that point in time the preacher had an estimated net worth of $27 million dollars, which was 200 times more than the $29,640 average annual income of the people in his hometown and ministry location. And as all this information came out to the public, people were flocking to social media to criticize and accuse. Of course, I was so tempted to join the choir of rock-throwers.

I can admit that I don't agree with the preacher's methods; I'm not a follower of his teachings or reader of his books. Nevertheless, it would be unfair of me to assume that all that he has done is bad—to write him off as evil or fraudulent.

It is very possible that he has won more people to Christ than I. I have no doubts that his ministry has created more jobs than I have with mine. His messages have inspired and encouraged hundreds of thousands, possibly millions across the globe. And while researching I discovered that his ministry has donated way more than sixty million dollars to help the poor, at home and abroad.

Yet I still wanted to judge him (and I had Bible verses to support those judgments.) However, to judge him is to bring judgement on myself.

Oh my gosh, yes, I want to ask all famous prosperity gospel televangelists to stop asking for so much money. I want them to move out of their million-dollar mansions and turn them into shelters for the homeless. I wish they would sell their fancy cars and give the money to the widows and the orphans in their congregations. And I want them to stop promoting the message of Western prosperity that makes us look cheap in the eyes of the world.

In spite of that, *it is I who needs to stop.*

Instead of demanding that they give more to the poor, I should give more of myself.

I don't have a mansion but I do have food on my table three meals a day. So even though I can't feed hundreds, I could probably feed a few on a weekly basis. When I get invited to preach and travel and receive an honorarium, maybe I should ask Jesus if I can give it back to the needy in whichever city I am in, instead of spending half of it at the airport on the way home.

You see, the problem is not wealth; the problem is the love of money.

And I love money, so I have a problem with wealth.

As John wrote: "*If anyone has material possessions and sees a brother or sister in need but has no pity on them, how can the love of God be in that person? Dear children, let us not love with words or speech but with actions and in truth.*"[2]

It sounds ridiculous to me that a preacher "needs" a sixty-five-million-dollar airplane to preach the gospel. But it might also seem ridiculous to a father of twelve in Niger that I would "need" an iPad to preach my sermons or the newest iMac to write this book.

There is nothing wrong with growing your finances. It's great when Christians are wealthy (because that should mean more money to fund the mission of Christ.) Nevertheless, there is a line for how much money we as leaders should spend on ourselves. I don't know where the line is, but it might be somewhere between people going to bed hungry and pastors going to bed inside their own airplanes.

Does that sound fair? I need your help figuring out this one.

My wife and I enjoy giving, tithing, prospering, and having nice things. God has been good to us and we are extremely grateful. I just hope that we keep moving toward being *givers* instead of *getters*, *creators* instead of *consumers*, and *lovers* instead of *takers*.

Yes, it is difficult to "defend" our faith when stories like these go viral. And trust me, I am all for the body of Christ returning to the way of the cross and the way of the first-century church. But maybe I need to focus less on how these other ministers spend their money and instead focus on Jesus' invitation to me: *"You lack one thing: go, sell all that you have and give to the poor, and you will have treasure in heaven; and come, follow me."*[3]

These words haunt my selfish soul. They were spoken by Jesus to a rich young ruler, and the Bible says that Jesus loved that rich young ruler.

America is a rich young nation, and Jesus loves this rich young nation.

If you have food in your fridge, clothes on your back, a roof over your head, and a place to sleep, you are richer than 75 percent of the world. And Jesus loves you.

It's because Jesus loved that rich young ruler (as well as He loves us) that He invites us to a greater surrender. The invitation to the rich young ruler was not so that he would go from wealthy to impoverished, but from slave to free; from being a puppet to his possessions to being a follower of Christ, who owns his possessions for the sake of the kingdom.

There is something I have discovered during my eight years of pastoring in Raleigh, North Carolina: people in America have enough of God to not need Him anymore.

There is another thing I have discovered in my eight years of living in Raleigh, North Carolina; I have to fight this temptation just the same.

Maybe it was not just the fact that the rich young ruler had to give all his money away, but also that he had to give it to people who could give him nothing in return. I know that I like giving when there is some measure of kickback. Even if the return is not the full value, I want something— anything! A picture on Facebook saying that I'm so generous, a donation receipt so I can get a few bucks back in taxes, a kiss and a hug and a thank you letter…anything!

So I know this from experience: the easiest thing is to accommodate the words of God to fit our lifestyle instead of surrendering our lifestyle to accommodate the words of God. And that is precisely what the rich young ruler did. He knew the law, he obeyed the law, and he had a heart to please God. But he lacked one thing, and because of his great wealth, he chose to not accept the Rabbi's invitation. *What a shame*, because he was one of the few people outside of the twelve disciples who had a direct invitation from Christ to follow Him in the journey.

As the rich young ruler was walking away, Jesus said, "*It is easier for a camel to go through the eye of a needle than for a rich man to enter the kingdom of God.*"[4]

The disciples (understandably) were astonished by these words and asked Him, "*Then who can be saved?*" Jesus replied, "*With people it is impossible, but not with God; for all things are possible with God.*"[5]

What is this "impossible thing for us" that becomes, "possible with God?"

Well, it's not, "I can have whatever I want because 'all things are possible with God!'"

Quite the contrary actually.

The desire in the heart of Jesus is for us to be able to say, "I can give away everything. Be saved from *mammon*. Yes, it is impossible for me but not impossible for God."

How bizarre that we have turned this very statement into the prayer and declaration we use to ask for success and possessions.

"I can have a new car, because nothing is impossible with God."

"I can get the hot wife, because nothing is impossible with God."

"I can be Instagram famous, because nothing is impossible with God."

It is true that those things are also possible with God, but reading these words in context is necessary. Jesus was speaking to the moment. A wealthy, godly man had just rejected a direct invitation to give his possessions away, and Jesus was aware that this would be hard for anyone in any scenario, so He reminded us again of a supernatural equation.

Impossible + You and I = Possible with God

Society and culture are begging us to be more successful; bigger, better, and richer is the ultimate goal for those who are hungry for recognition. Our materialism is gasping for more and our vanity is desperate for exclusivity.

Despite that, it's possible, with God, to surrender lands and titles, to give away our time and our best efforts, and to be generous with our money, our talents, and our hands. We can choose, in Christ, to give it all away.

It's the privilege of crucifixion.

And in this gospel of generosity we surrender our possessions to the possessor of all. I know this might not be good news to the rich but it is definitely good news to the poor.[6]

John D. Rockefeller, the Ohio native who started Standard Oil, was a billionaire in the early 1900s, and he's still considered the richest person in modern history. When a reporter asked him, "How much money is enough?" he responded, "Just a little bit more."

When what we already have is *never enough*, then *never enough* will become our god. This idol must come down. Let us not lack that one thing.

Before his current job as prophet/comedian/host of the *The Late Show with Stephen Colbert* on CBS, Colbert had a TV show on basic cable, on which he said,

> If this is going to be a Christian nation that doesn't help the poor, either we have to pretend that Jesus was just as selfish as we are, or we've got to acknowledge that He commanded us to love the poor and serve the needy without condition and then admit that we just don't want to do it.[7]

I admit that most of the time I don't want to do it. But I want to change, so I'll start with forgiveness. I forgive every church leader who has asked for millions of dollars to expand their personal kingdoms. And I forgive myself for pretending like I wouldn't do the same.

Notes

1. Charles Spurgeon, *John Ploughman's Talks* (New Kensington, PA: Whitaker House, 2012), 101.
2. 1 John 3:17–18 NIV.
3. Mark 10:21.
4. Mark 10:25.
5. Verses 26–27
6. See Luke 4:18.
7. Stephen Colbert, "Jesus Is a Liberal Democrat," *The Colbert Report*, December 16, 2010, http://www.cc.com/video-clips/m38gcf/the-colbert-report-jesus-is-a-liberal-democrat.

34

HUMANITY

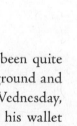

"Racism is man's gravest threat to man—the maximum
of hatred for a minimum of reason, the maximum of cruelty
for a minimum of thinking."[1]
—*Abraham Joshua Heschel*

I was scheduled to preach on Sunday, July 10, 2016. It had been quite
a week. On Tuesday, Alton Sterling had been pinned to the ground and
fatally shot by police at a Baton Rouge convenience store. On Wednesday,
Philando Castile was shot by a policeman as he reached for his wallet
during a "routine" traffic stop, as his girlfriend and her four-year-old daughter looked on. Then, on Thursday, five Dallas police officers were killed by a
sniper while protecting a Black Lives Matter protest march.

Tensions were high, opinions were loud and scary, politicians with different agendas were using the collective fear to sell their agendas, and a
multitude of Christians were being nasty to each other on social media.

I shared a sermon about being family, about holding hands and listening to each other without trying to control what we say or feel. I then gave
the microphone to a black couple and told them to just share what they
experience in their day-to-day life in such a charged atmosphere. They were
honest, humble, and inviting. Then, a white veteran from the church asked
forgiveness for the sins of his race. He was honest, humble, and inviting.

Then, we prayed together for the police and for the families that were affected, and we hugged it out, right there and then.

It was so hopeful to see the family of God speaking life to each other—black people and white people, Latinos and Asians, young and old, boomers and millennials. It was a manifestation of what the church truly is, and what it could provide for the world in moments like these. It was not about covering the truth with a cute and safe church moment; it was about facing the facts head-on and allowing the ferocious love of God to initiate solutions.

Honestly, I was tempted to just preach about something else that day. I felt so inadequate to share. I'm not black. I'm not a cop. I felt like just another voice in the chaotic narrative. And still I know that my opinions will not have the solution to this terrible, systemic problem. My perspective on what happens is random and inconclusive.

I know little, but God knows what we need to do. And I suggest we do it.

We can start with *"Let love be genuine. Abhor what is evil; hold fast to what is good. Love one another with brotherly affection. Outdo one another in showing honor."*[2]

Then move on to *"Bless those who persecute you; bless and do not curse them. Rejoice with those who rejoice, weep with those who weep. Live in harmony with one another."*[3]

And finish with: *"Never be wise in your own sight. Repay no one evil for evil, but give thought to do what is honorable in the sight of all. If possible, so far as it depends on you, live peaceably with all."*[4]

This is the voice of God in the writings of Paul in Romans 12.

It's the perfect Judge asking us for the courage to *not* judge. It's the loving Savior asking us for the grace to *not* get into *right or wrong* spitting contests. It's the perfect Healer asking us to be hands and feet that are drenched in compassion—for each other.

God the Father is asking us to be Jesus to the hurting in our nation.

Jesus who washed the feet of Judas.

Jesus who defended the oppressed.

Jesus who forgave the people who murdered Him.

Jesus who died unjustly as a criminal.

We all know that after every act of violence that goes viral, we are exposed to different thoughts and responses. Pastors, politicians, teachers, and soccer-moms enter the debate and chose sides according to their experiences, biases, and beliefs.

I know you're tired of it (I know I am) so maybe there's a better way, a different response—one that starts and ends with us.

I believe these occasions demand that we take responsibility for our part, because if we are not part of the solution then we're part of the problem. The hour has also come to deal with our own racism—that bit of "harmless" prejudice, the slight disdain for the people of another color, culture, gender, sexual orientation, or religion. True healing of bigotry starts with the acknowledgment that the most dangerous racist in our lives is the one raging on the inside.

Scientifically, humanity is composed of exactly one race. Although the world has different ethnicities, citizenships, geographies, and cultures, all human beings are nearly identical genetically. The genetic distinctions that reflect variation in physical appearance across the human race involve just 0.01 percent of our genes.[5] And we were all made in the image of God.

I am.

Every victim of police shooting in America was.

Every protester and every police officer is.

And so are you.

Scripture tells us, *"Words like Jewish and non-Jewish, religious and irreligious, insider and outsider, uncivilized and uncouth, slave and free, mean nothing. From now on everyone is defined by Christ, everyone is included in Christ."*[6]

And this Christ experienced racism in his lifetime. When Nathaniel was told about the Messiah for the first time, he responded with the question, *"Can anything good come out of Nazareth?"*[7] This statement distinguished the people of Nazareth as lesser, inferior, and bad.

Jesus was also judged based on His social status. They called Him *"the carpenter's son,"*[8] as if to say poor, uneducated, lesser, inferior, and bad.

He was born in little Bethlehem, lived as a minority in the Roman Empire, and was murdered as a criminal on a cross. He was treated as poor, uneducated, lesser, inferior, and bad.

I know He understands the struggle, and I'm sure He's the only solution. So whatever the question is, love is the answer. Not our version of love…Jesus' version; the version that favors understanding, community, and kindness; the version that turns enemies into friends and strangers into family; the version that forgives police officers for their brutality and acknowledges the pain of those who have been brutalized; the version that believes the best about anyone who has ever used the hashtags #BlackLivesMatter and #BlueLivesMatter.

Compassion is not just an emotion that makes us feel pity, it's a godly invitation. It's the call to do it like God Himself did it—to draw closer to the "other," embrace their experience, and die for their benefit.

As Heidi Baker likes to say, "Love looks like something!"

What is it going to look like after this chapter is finished?

For me it looks like cooking a Puerto Rican meal for my African-American neighbor while we talk alongside my European wife about family, race, relations, and police shootings. It looks like praying together with police officers in our church community and extending a hand of friendship. It looks like admitting to the systematic racism that burdens our black families and standing courageously with them. For us, the church of Jesus, it looks like a combination of hundreds of little acts of love.

It would be good to carve the words of the late Nelson Mandela into our minds.

No one is born hating another person because of the color of his skin, or his background, or his religion. People must learn to hate, and if they can learn to hate, they can be taught to love, for love comes more naturally to the human heart than its opposite.[9]

We are ready to learn.

So let us open the table of communion at our gatherings. Let us have a dialogue founded on love instead of opinions. And let us listen to understand, not to respond. And remember that the "love your neighbor as yourself" has no small print at the bottom putting conditions on the statement.

We could spend hours and hours talking about what the white police or the black community should do…but that's the easy part. The difficult (less attractive part) is to take the kingdom of God approach: deal with the sin on the inside, take the log out of our eyes, repent for the hate in our hearts, and drop the stone of racism from our hands.

It's easy to tweet 140 characters about police brutality or *black on black* *crime*. It's easy to share judgment on Facebook about criminals or rioters. It's harder to pray, harder to love, and harder to understand.

Let's do the hard things.

Notes

1. Abraham J. Heschel, *The Insecurity of Freedom: Essays on Human Existence* (New York: Farrar, Straus, and Giroux, 1963), 86.
2. Romans 12:9–10.
3. Verses 14–16.
4. Verses 16–18.
5. S. C. Cameron and S. M. Wycoff, "The destructive nature of the term race: growing beyond a false paradigm," *Journal of Counseling and Development*, 1998, 76:277–285.
6. Colossians 3:11 MSG.
7. John 1:46.
8. Matthew 13:55, see also Mark 6:3.
9. Nelson Mandela, *Long Walk to Freedom* (New York: Back Bay Books, Little, Brown and Company, 1994), 622.

35

NO US AND THEM

*"My first allegiance is not to a flag, a country, or a man.
It's not to democracy or blood. It's to a king and a kingdom."*[1]
—*Derek Webb*

I'm a proud Puerto Rican. Some of you thought I was Mexican by looking at my profile picture…and that's okay. Because I'm also proud to be a Latino and I love my Mexican brothers.

At least once a month someone assumes that I'm a Muslim Arab. They give me a nod and say, *"Salam Alaikum"* (Peace be unto you) and with joy I reply, *"Wa-Alaikum-Salaam"* (And unto you, peace). Then I explain to them that I'm not from Jordan but born and raised in San Juan.

I carry a US passport. My great-grandparents became American citizens in 1917 through the Jones-Shafroth Act, and now I get to live and vote in America.

I'm also married to what could be the whitest person you have ever seen. My gorgeous wife, Catherine Rachel, was born and raised in England and is pure Anglo-Saxon (with no traces in her family tree but pure Anglo-Saxon). That's probably why my sons are the two whitest-looking kids in our church. Half-British, half-Puerto-Rican, bilinguals, and raised in the USA.

As a family, we are adopting an African daughter. Our Ethiopian princess is (and will be) black and proud. We will raise her to love her culture, speak her native tongue, and add her flare to our United Nations dinner table.

The pastors in our church are a mix of Canadian, Nigerian, British, Australian, Pakistani, and American. And if I tell you about our staff and volunteers, we could easily add another ten nationalities to the list.

As Father Gregory Boyle says, "There is no us and them, there's just us."[2]

This quote realigns me every time I'm tempted to draw lines and separate from those who are different than me; but I think the gospel invitation goes even deeper than that. It goes from knowing that we are an *us* to choosing the *us* above ourselves. As Jesus said about Himself (while inviting us to the same level), *"Greater love has no one than this, that someone lay down his life for his friends."*[3]

Welcome to the ministry of reconciliation.

It is yours in this lifetime, according to 2 Corinthians 5.

It's the breaking down of the walls of hostility that Paul talks about in Galatians 2.

It's the multicolored wisdom of God, expressed in a multicolored people.

And if the people of God would have accepted this invitation, then there would be more Samaritans alive today.

I say this because during the time of Jesus, they were a people despised. And as of January 1, 2015, the living population of Samaritans in the world is 777.[4] They have been decimated because for so long they were considered a lesser race, a lesser religion, and a lesser group of people. But Jesus engaged them continually with honor.

In Luke 10:25 an expert in the law stood up and tested Jesus (bad idea). He said to Him, *"Teacher, what shall I do to inherit eternal life?"* or in other words, "What can I do to go to heaven?"

In verse 26, and in full Jesus style, He replied to his question with two questions:

1. *"What is written in the Law?"* (Tell me what you know.)

2. *"How do you read it?"* (Tell me how you interpret it.)

In verse 27, the lawyer quotes from Deuteronomy and Leviticus: *"You shall love the Lord your God with all your heart and with all your soul and with all your strength and with all your mind, and your neighbor as yourself."*

A round of applause for knowing the Scriptures so well.

In verse 28, the Word of God said to him, *"You have answered correctly; do this, and you will live."*

But the man, desiring to justify himself (bad idea again) asked Jesus in verse 29, *"Who is my neighbor?"* or, in other words, "Who shall I stand with? And where do I draw the line?"

Jesus replies with a parable; a story that was intended (in love) to offend the mind in order to reveal the heart.

And this is what the Way, the Truth, and the Life said,

"A man was going down from Jerusalem to Jericho, and he fell among robbers, who stripped him and beat him and departed, leaving him half dead. Now by chance a priest was going down that road, and when he saw him he passed by on the other side. So likewise a Levite, when he came to the place and saw him, passed by on the other side. But a Samaritan, as he journeyed, came to where he was, and when he saw him, he had compassion. He went to him and bound up his wounds, pouring on oil and wine. Then he set him on his own animal and brought him to an inn and took care of him. And the next day he took out two denarii and gave them to the innkeeper, saying, 'Take care of him, and whatever more you spend, I will repay you when I come back.' Which of these three, do you think, proved to be a neighbor to the man who fell among the robbers?" He said, "The one who showed him mercy." And Jesus said to him, "You go, and do likewise."[5]

Notice how hard it was for the lawyer to admit something good about the Samaritan and answer with the actual words, *"The Samaritan."*

Notice also how Jesus told him to be like the Samaritan he could not even acknowledge.

This parable would have been challenging enough for the lawyer if the Samaritan was the one beaten up on the side of the road and all Jesus was asking him to do was help the poor bastard. However, He used that example not just to say, *be kind to your despised neighbor*, but also to say, *learn from them!*

As Dr. Martin Luther King Jr. preached on this verse the day before he died, "And so the first question that the priest asked, the first question that the Levite asked was, 'If I stop to help this man, what will happen to me?' But then the Good Samaritan came by, and he reversed the question: 'If I do not stop to help this man, what will happen to him?'"[6]

Can we ask this again, "What will happen to the undocumented worker from Central America if we don't stop to help them? What will happen to the hordes of refugees in the Middle East if we don't stop to help them? What will happen to homeless veterans if we don't stop to help them?"

And even more than that, we need to ask, "How can we relate to them so we can learn from them?"

This is humility personified.

I believe it to be a good thing to cherish the land God blessed us with. We need to appreciate our culture, learn our history, and respect our people. But Jesus couldn't care less about our patriotism—the whole point of the gospel was to include everyone. It's the original promise to Abraham, "Through you all peoples on earth will be blessed."[7] That includes communists and Iranians, the Muslims and the French, and even us Puerto Ricans! In His eyes, every country is the greatest country; every person is His favorite person. At the cross, we all become His number ones, and no matter your nationality, color, religion, politics, or hairstyle, you have been loved into the greatest family.

Nationalism is a deceptive evil that needs to be confronted as a deceptive evil. Sure, it works for history books and competitive Olympic Games, but it does not work for making disciples of all nations. It does not fit the picture of Revelation: *"An eternal gospel to proclaim to those who live on earth, to every nation and tribe and language and people."*[8]

We can't be the bride of Christ *and* concubines of Caesar. We can't choose the empires of this world *and* the ways of His kingdom. We can't prioritize a superpower over God's humility and fire. As Stanley Hauerwas wrote, "The church is constituted as a new people who have been gathered from the nations to remind the world that we are in fact one people."[9]

A few years before moving from Puerto Rico to Raleigh, I visited a church in Pasadena, California. The people in attendance had a sincere desire for the things of God. The speakers at the conference were full of wisdom and humility, but I just could not get over the one-million-dollar chandelier in the foyer. Every time I walked in the building, that monstrosity of greed looked at me and mocked me. Note that it was not the current church that had spent the money putting the chandelier there. It was a cult with a following of a few hundred thousand people that previously inhabited the auditorium, which had been part of their headquarters before their leader surrendered his life to Jesus. The building ended up in the hands of the current church family (which is a cool story for another day).

But I sounded like Judas every time I walked in the foyer, "This could have been sold at a high price and given to the poor."[10]

And you know what? Both Judas and I were right. But saying the right thing with the wrong heart automatically makes it the wrong thing. So once again, God challenged my attitude. Not because He's a nitpicker, more because He's a good Father, and good fathers discipline their children.

I was on the floor in a moment of worship, pretending to be holier than others, when the Lord asked me, "Will you give your life for the USA?"

"God," I said, while looking up to the ceiling confused, "You know I've been called to Africa, to Latin America, and to the poorest of the poor. Why would I ever give my life for America?"

He replied, "Why would I send you to Africa and Latin America, which you are naturally inclined to glorify, and not bring you to the US, which you are naturally inclined to criticize?"

"I get that, God," I replied. "But do You really have to answer every question with a question?" and, "Is this even You talking? I might be going crazy."

Still, I knew that if I was going crazy, it was the right kind of crazy.

That day I discovered one of my life mottos, via the great Henri Nouwen: "For [Jesus] there are no countries to be conquered, no ideologies to be imposed, and no people to be dominated. There are only children, women, and men to be loved."[11]

I knew right then and there that it was for me to live in America, and for me to preach to the American church. Today, some of my best friends, my favorite TV shows, and my greatest influencers come from this glorious land. It has been eight years of following the advice from the apostle Paul when he said, *"I have become all things to all people, that by all means I might save some."*[12]

It has also been eight years of realizing that I have been called to challenge the nationalism in America, while also letting America challenge the nationalist in me.

These wonderful people have so much to give to me and I have so much to learn from them. Being aware of things that need correcting doesn't automatically turn us into the correctors...most of the time, as the great American evangelist Billy Graham was quoted as saying, "It is the Holy Spirit's job to convict, God's job to judge, and my job to love."[13]

Let the loving continue.

Admitting that we are lost is the first step to embracing the rescue of Jesus. And for us here in America, Canada, and the UK, admitting that Western Christianity has made us captives to our nationalism will help us rediscover the Christ that saves Muslims, Buddhists, atheists, and Christians with the same love and conviction.

As Paul warned the people in the capital city of the Roman Empire, *"I appeal to you, brothers, to watch out for those who cause divisions and create obstacles contrary to the doctrine that you have been taught; avoid them."*[14]

The doctrine taught by Paul was one of inclusion; of accepting the Gentiles as people grafted into the vine. In turn, we need to avoid the natural inclination to value our ethnicity above others. We need to avoid the obstacles created by nationalistic rhetoric and an overpowering perspective—because the most ridiculous thing we could do would be to utilize a faith that included us Gentiles as a tool to treat others like uninvited non-members. That would be a direct contradiction to the message that reached us.

So let the loving continue.

Notes

1. Derek W. Webb, "A King & a Kingdom," *Mockingbird*, INO Records, 2005.
2. Interview with Gregory Boyle. "Preventing Gang Violence: Why Kids Become Violent," *PsychAlive*. https://www.psychalive.org/preventing-gang-violence-why-kids-become-violent/. (Accessed March 29, 2017.)
3. John 15:13.
4. A. V. "Who are the Samaritans and why is their future uncertain?" *The Economist*, October 18, 2016, http://www.economist.com/blogs/economist-explains/2016/10/economist-explains-14. (Accessed March 28, 2017.)
5. Luke 10:30–37.
6. Martin Luther King Jr., "I've Been to the Mountaintop," sermon delivered on April 3, 1968, in Memphis, Tennessee, http://kingencyclopedia.stanford.edu/encyclopedia/documentsentry/ive_been_to_the_mountaintop/. (Accessed March 27, 2017.)
7. See Genesis 22:18.
8. Revelation 14:6.
9. Stanley Hauerwas, *In Good Company: The Church as Polis* (Notre Dame, IN: Notre Dame Press, 1995).
10. See Matthew 26:9; Mark 14:5; John 12:5.
11. Henry Nouwen, *Peacework: Prayer, Resistance, Community* (Maryknoll, NY: Orbis Books, 2005), 94.
12. 1 Corinthians 9:22.
13. Sandra Chambers, "Billy Graham: A Faithful Witness," *Charisma News*, November 7, 2013, http://www.charismanews.com/us/41684-billy-graham-a-faithful-witness. (Accessed March 29, 2017.)
14. Romans 16:17.

36

GENTILE LIVES MATTER

> "The ultimate measure of a man is not where he stands in
> moments of comfort and convenience, but where he stands at
> times of challenge and controversy."[1]
> —*Martin Luther King Jr.*

Don't imply the apostle Peter had an issue with racism. Let the apostle Paul do that.

In public.

And forever recorded in the Bible.

This is Saul vs. Simon in Galatians 2:11–13:

But when Cephas [Peter] came to Antioch, I opposed him to his face, because he stood condemned. For before certain men came from James, he was eating with the Gentiles; but when they came he drew back and separated himself, fearing the circumcision party. And the rest of the Jews acted hypocritically along with him, so that even Barnabas was led astray by their hypocrisy.

Paul called his friend out for being a condemned, hypocritical leader who would not relate to the Gentiles (uncircumcised) in Antioch. Peter enjoyed the privilege of being Jewish, but Paul challenged him to use that privilege for good.

Do you see racism in Peter's actions? Maybe the official definition of the word will help explain what I'm trying to say about him.

Rac·ism (noun): "The belief that all members of each race possess characteristics or abilities specific to that race, especially so as to distinguish it as inferior or superior to another race or races."

That sounds a bit like Peter, a man born and raised in the belief that the Jewish people were chosen, special, and superior, a man who had read the stories of Jehovah ordering the destruction of the women and children who were not the seed of Abraham, and a man who had sung the psalms that celebrated Israel's place of favor.

And then that man spent three years with the Jewish Messiah. He was chosen by that Messiah to be the leader of his group. He saw that Messiah ascend to the heavens, and he received the very Spirit that the Messiah sent. Yes, Peter the apostle had every reason to believe that his race was superior to the other races. He had read God's Word, he had met God's Word, and he was full of God's Word.

And his interpretation was that Gentiles did not matter as much as he did.

Not the Samaritans.

Not the Greeks.

And definitely not the Romans.

I'm not judging Peter here. God knows I have my own racism to deal with. There are lies on the inside that tell me that *Christian* is superior, *US citizen* is superior, *Latino* is superior, *I* am superior. And just like Peter, I need to revamp my perspective.

The Rock had his worldview confronted in a revelation. We read in Acts 10 that Peter fell into a trance. He saw the skies open up and something that looked like a huge blanket lowered by ropes at its four corners settled on the ground. Every kind of animal and reptile and bird was on it.

And there came a voice to him: "Rise, Peter; kill and eat." But Peter said, "By no means, Lord; for I have never eaten anything that is common or unclean."[2]

You see, this was God using Peter's prejudice to speak to Peter's heart, because it was Peter who saw the Gentiles as a lesser animal race. In verse 15, the voice came a second time: *"What God has made clean, do not call common."*

This happened three times, and then the blanket was pulled back up into the sky.

This event occurred so that Peter would be open to the idea of going into the house of a Roman centurion named Cornelius, who had been prepared by God to hear the gospel and to be filled with the Holy Spirit.

I always wondered why God did not just tell the good news directly to Cornelius. Now I have a holy suspicion: God wanted to save Cornelius, but He also wanted to save Peter. He wanted to save the fisherman-preacher from a life lost in good news only meant for his people, his race, and his pre-selected few. God was confronting Peter's hypocrisy and racism. I have no doubt that God loved him as he was, but there was something better available for him.

Thank goodness Peter was obedient to the invitation from heaven. He went to Cornelius' house, and once there, he began his sermon, saying, *"Truly I understand that God shows no partiality."*[3]

He seemed to truly understand.

Although he later forgot.

Because thirty-something years later, Paul is correcting him for showing partiality afresh.

When non-Christian Jews in Jerusalem heard that Peter, a prominent church leader, was eating with Gentiles in Antioch, they would not only turn away from the church but also become actively hostile toward the church for tolerating such a practice. Confronted by these concerns for his home church and its mission to the Jews, Peter acted against his own better judgment. He separated himself from the Gentiles.[4] All the Jewish believers in Antioch were subservient to Peter's authority and followed his example. As a result, the church was split into racial factions: Jews were divided from Gentiles.

These actions were inconsistent with their convictions about the truth of the gospel. Yet they all were more influenced by their common racial identity as Jews than by their new nature in Christ. Déjà vu.

We know that Peter was a champion of the faith who gave his life for Jesus. He was brave, humble, determined, and radical. Church history tells us that he was crucified upside down, because he did not consider himself worthy of dying in the same manner that his Savior died.

Jesus was right about Peter, he rocked.

But he had a struggle, just like we do.

That struggle was confronted by Paul, the apostle to the Gentiles, a man who had no fear to tell each race, each town, each gathering, that Gentiles are important to God. Gentiles were now chosen and included, and they were worth dying for.

Of course, Paul knew that all lives mattered, but God gave him a specific mission: #GentileLivesMatter.

I'm glad Paul followed the leading of Jesus for his life.

If he hadn't, not many of us would have heard the good news.

You see, full of the Holy Spirit in Acts 2:17, it was Simon Peter who announced: *"In the last days it shall be, God declares, that I will pour out my Spirit on all flesh."*

Peter knew that God's plan was for everyone to receive the Spirit, however, that belief demanded intentional relating and connecting to Gentiles in order for them to receive it. It was more than just saying the words, it also included being in proximity with them.

Paul was incredible at this. And so was Peter…when he wasn't afraid of what others would do or say.

Notes

1. Martin Luther King Jr., *A Gift of Love: Sermons from Strength to Love and Other Preachings* (Boston: Beacon Press, 1963), 27.
2. Acts 10:13–14.
3. Acts 10:34.
4. See Galatians 2:12.

37

HOLY POLITICS

"The cross is not a detour or a hurdle on the way to the kingdom,
nor is it even the way to the kingdom; it is the kingdom come."[1]
—*John Howard Yoder*

You know why people talk about politics so much? Because God placed that value in our hearts…oh yes, He did!

You see, politics are not the spawn of Satan or the work of the flesh. Satan has certainly used politics in the past, and our flesh has certainly fallen for its traps. Still, politics are important, godly important—and Jesus is the master politician.

You've noticed that I'm into definitions, so here's the definition of the word.

Politics (noun): "The activities associated with the governance of a country or other area, especially the debate or conflict among individuals or parties having or hoping to achieve power."

We can all agree that it is important to attend to *the activities associated with the governance of a country or any other area*. Where we disagree (and turn ugly) is in *the debate or conflict among individuals or parties having or hoping to achieve power.*

God is concerned with the wellbeing of humankind (in every country, religion, and race). The problem is that we have reduced politics to what we like (in every country, religion, and race) as opposed to being guided by the gospel.

The core problem lies in the *hoping to achieve power*. It's like we're all in the *Game of Thrones* and Jesus is the only one free from the coming winter.

In the past, I have fallen under the illusion that Jesus is not political, but the reality is that He is the most political of all. As Eugene Peterson wrote, "The gospel of Jesus Christ is more political than anyone imagines, but in a way that no one guesses."[2]

It all started way back when Jesus, *"who, though he was in the form of God, did not count equality with God a thing to be grasped, but emptied himself, taking the form of a servant."*[3] The highest chose to be the lowest. The powerful chose to be the helper. And He was radically active in the activities associated with the governance of a country or other area, especially the debate or conflict among individuals or parties having or hoping to achieve power.

He did it differently than all the other religious and political leaders in history, but make no mistake, Jesus is the King of Kings and the Lord of Lords, and He has a singular agenda in place.

Multiple times, Jesus began His kingdom announcements by saying, "You have heard it said…" and off He went debating the ways of the religious age. By touching lepers, empowering women, and healing on the Sabbath, Jesus was challenging the climate of His time. We can think of the Jewish leaders as the conservatives and the Roman rulers as the liberals—they both had a part in killing Him, and they both desperately needed (need) His dominion.

Yes, Jesus cares about politics.

But not our kind of politics.

Our liberal and conservative agendas are in opposition to the agenda of Christ. We want to make it work…but it just doesn't. Neither the elephant nor the donkey can represent the Lamb. It's up to us ambassadors not to create a new way to be politically Christian but to follow the politics of

Christ. The Right and the Left will always miss an unmissable component. Their ultimate goal is to win, rule, dominate, govern, and control.

They seek power; Jesus seeks to serve.

And He told us to do the same.

Also, every political agenda on earth has an opponent. The politics of Jesus came to eliminate enemies by making them into something else. And He told us to do the same:

"Pray for those who persecute you" (Matthew 5:44).

"Pray for those who abuse you" (Luke 6:28).

"Love your enemies" (Matthew 5:44).

"Welcome the stranger" (see Matthew 25:35–40).

"Make disciples of all nations" (Matthew 28:19).

If we choose the politics of Christ, then a new reformation can begin. And no matter how we vote, we get to surrender to His strategy of grace.

If we want the kingdom to come, then we need the King to rule. If we want *on earth as it is in heaven*, then we need to honor heaven's priorities. The church has spent two thousand years electing Trumps and Clintons, Reagans and Obamas; it might be time to choose the agenda of the Christ we claim as Monarch.

He doesn't need our votes, but He does want our hearts.

Will He get our alliance?

Notes

1. John Howard Yoder, *The Politics of Jesus* (Grand Rapids, MI: Wm. B. Eerdmans, 1994), 51.
2. Eugene Peterson, *Reversed Thunder: The Revelation of John and the Praying Imagination* (New York: HarperOne, 1991), 117.
3. Philippians 2:6–7.

38

LIBERAL OR CONSERVATIVE?

"When you get the government involved with religious programs…it's like mixing horse manure with ice cream. It won't do much to the manure but it will really mess up the ice cream."[1]
—*Tony Campolo*

A 2012 study found that US Christians on both sides of the political divide believe Jesus is more compassionate than they are.

PTL.

Liberal Christians tend to believe that Jesus is more conservative than they are on moral issues, while conservative Christians believe He is more liberal. However, the survey and study from the Proceedings of the National Academy of Sciences additionally showed that "liberal and conservative Christians also tend to believe that the matters most important to Jesus are the same ones most important to them."[2]

I'm glad there's a study to prove this, but I'm sure Facebook and Twitter have corroborated this already. Most of us are convinced that Jesus would vote like we vote, but claiming Jesus for one side or the other is absolute foolishness. He rules outside of all our boxes, religious and political alike. Assuming that He thinks like us proves that our opinions are our lord, not Him.

When we pray, "Let Your kingdom come," we are likewise praying, "Let my kingdom go." So, in order to deconstruct the lie that lives inside all of us, which screams, "I'M RIGHT," here are ten verses that prove Jesus could be a liberal and a conservative.

The first five are liberal:

1. *"Blessed are the peacemakers, for they shall be called sons of God"* (Matthew 5:9).

No to war.

Simple.

2. *"Love your enemies"* (Matthew 5:44).

Yes.

All your enemies.

3. *"Again I tell you, it is easier for a camel to go through the eye of a needle than for a rich man to enter the kingdom of God"* (Matthew 19:24).

Be careful with prosperity.

Give to the poor.

4. *"Render to Caesar the things that are Caesar's, and to God the things that are God's"* (Matthew 22:21).

Don't complain paying taxes.

Be cool with the separation of church and state.

5. *"For I was hungry and you gave me food, I was thirsty and you gave me drink, I was a stranger and you welcomed me, I was naked and you clothed me, I was sick and you visited me, I was in prison and you came to me"* (Matthew 25:35–36).

Give to the needy.

Welcome refugees.

The next five are conservative:

1. *"And Zacchaeus stood up and said to the Lord, 'Behold, Lord, the half of my goods I give to the poor. And if I have defrauded anyone of anything, I restore it fourfold'"* (Luke 19:8).

Giving is voluntary, not forced.

2. "[Jesus] *answered. 'Have you not read that he who created them from the beginning made them male and female, and said, "Therefore a man shall leave his father and his mother and hold fast to his wife, and the two shall become one flesh"?'"* (Matthew 19:4–5).

No divorce.

Man and woman marriage.

3. "*Sin no more, that nothing worse may happen to you*" (John 5:14).

Sin is serious.

Beware of its consequences.

4. "*And if your right hand causes you to sin, cut it off and throw it away. For it is better that you lose one of your members than that your whole body go into hell*" (Matthew 5:30).

Easy, Jesus.

Easy.

5. "*I am the way, and the truth, and the life*" (John 14:6).

Not "a" way but "*the*" way.

The ultimate truth, in love.

The words of Jesus could be interpreted as both liberal and conservative in one single verse. Seriously, the main theme of this book proves just that! When He saved the woman who was caught in the act of adultery, He said to her, "*Neither do I condemn you* (liberal), *go, and from now on sin no more* (conservative)."[3]

So come on, church. We have to stop this ridiculous battle of trying to prove how much better we are at interpreting Scripture. We need to eliminate the small divisions of politics and focus on the greater works of Christ. We can be family…even while voting differently. *It's possible!* Just ask the disciples of Jesus. You had Matthew the tax collector (who worked for the Roman Empire) and Simon the Zealot (a terrorist who wanted to destroy that empire).

Jesus loved them both, chose them both, and empowered them both.

The key was *conversation*.

The need remains *honor*.

The time is *now*.

The issues of abortion, racial inequality, gun violence, and terrorism (and all the other issues we care about) are radically important. That is why Jesus came to save us. His gospel is the good news for all those involved and affected by these issues. If that's not the news you want to hear, then stick to BBC, CNN, or Fox, and leave the kingdom of God above it all. Because trust me (and I can guarantee you this one)…Jesus is already above it.

Tell them again, Brian Zahnd!

The kingdom of Christ is the most revolutionary politics—perhaps the only truly revolutionary politics—the world has ever seen. Unlike all other political agendas, the supreme value of the politics of Jesus is not power, but love. Jesus rejects the politics of power for the politics of love.[4]

Notes

1. Tony Campolo, *Speaking My Mind* (Nashville, TN: W Publishing Group, 2005).
2. Lee D. Ross, Yphtack Leikes, and Alexander G. Russell, "How Christians reconcile their personal political views and the teachings of their faith: Projection as a means of dissonance reduction," *Proceedings of the National Academy of Sciences of the United States of America*, pnas.org, March 6, 2012, http://www.pnas.org/content/109/10/3616.full. (Accessed March 28, 2017.)
3. John 8:11.
4. Brian Zahnd, "The Jesus Revolution," *Brian Zahnd* (blog), July 1, 2016, https://brianzahnd.com/2016/07/the-jesus-revolution/. (Accessed March 27, 2017.)

$$39$$

THE BATTLE OF FALSE RELIGIONS

"It doesn't matter what we think we're saying—
it's what others hear."[1]
—*Carl Medearis*

Six years ago I stood inside a church in a Muslim nation and shouted at the top of my lungs, *"Allahu Akbar!"* (God is great!). I said it because I wanted to be relevant to my raised-in-a-Muslim-culture audience, so I used this specific Arabic term that I had heard on TV.

And it was one of the dumbest things I have ever done.

My honest desire was connection. I had already been using, *"As-salamu Alaykum"* a well-known Arabic greeting that translates to, "peace be upon you," but mostly used as "hello." Everyone seemed to enjoy the fact that I said that one, so I decided I try some more. During my greeting in the first opportunity I had to preach, I said into the microphone, *"As-salamu Alaykum"* and with smiles on their faces everyone in attendance replied, *"Wa alaykumu s-salam."*

Boom!

I'm in.

Then, I confidently said my second rehearsed term, *"Allahu Akbar,"* which to me was, "God is Great" (because that's the yellow subtitle translation I had seen in Hollywood movies multiple times). But what they heard me saying was, "It's time for all of you to die!"

Boo.

I'm out.

You see, "*Allahu Akbar*" is an Islamic Arabic expression widely used by Muslims. It is commonly translated in English as "God is greater." Not everywhere in the Muslim world, but specifically in West Africa, this phrase is often associated with Islamic extremism; mostly because of its widespread usage by jihadists as a battle cry before committing an act of terrorism.

So yeah.

On my introduction in front of 100+ leaders, many who have been persecuted for preaching the gospel of Jesus, I gave a specific invitation to the killing of "infidels," aka everyone sitting in front of me. My translator paralyzed. The pastors in the front row lost their ability to blink. I assumed they had not heard me properly so I did what any good preacher would do in this scenario—I repeated it louder, "*Allaaahuuuu Akbarrrrr!*"

Absolute silence.

No one responded.

No one moved.

And thankfully, no one died.

I decided that their Arabic was not on par with mine, so I moved on with the Bible reading. When I later found out how incredibly naive that moment was, I decided to quit preaching forever! But the leaders there loved me through it and kept giving me opportunities to share more. (I just found a more appropriate introduction and stopped trusting Hollywood with my translations.)

Today, these people are partners—my African family, the mission I hold dearest to my heart. Because of their grace (and because of the magnitude of my ignorance), this story used to be funny.

But in 2015, people actually shouting "*Allahu Akbar!*" burned down that specific church building and tried to kill my friends. This place of worship where I have preached God's love is now in ruins. Homes where I ate and rested in are no more. Because of the hatred between Christians and Muslims in that area, my friends are running for their lives.

Crazy right? But this is the world we live in; and in it, Jesus is the only hope.

Note that I say *Jesus*, as in the-Savior-Teacher-born-in-Bethlehem Jesus. Not the Western make-me-rich-and-safe-and-successful Jesus.

I speak about the Son of God.

The Captain of salvation.

The Lord of Hosts.

The one who died for Osama and Obama and Osteen and Oprah and all the men who burned down my friends' church. Yes, that Jesus said to turn the other cheek. That Jesus said that the peacemakers would be the sons of God. *That* Jesus is the only hope.

The easiest thing for me is to hate the radical jihadists who did this; to hate Boko Haram, ISIS, and the Taliban. Yet I would be wise to learn from Jesus, to review the way He addressed His surroundings, and how He approached the issues of His lifetime.

I am no expert in politics or world issues, I just want to remind myself, as a Christian, of the things Christ did…of the words Christ said…and of the love Christ is.

The command is to love our Muslim neighbors and even our Muslim enemies.

As Nathan Hamm tweets every time we need reminding, "Love is Christlike, Islamophobia is antiChrist."[2]

Also, Jesus never addressed radical religions; He invited us to radical grace. He never judged the religion of the Samaritan people, He actually went out of His way to approach them, to teach them, and to love them. And if there are traces of Islamophobia in the West, wouldn't people in the Middle East have Christianophobia?

It's hard to admit, but in the name of God, Christians have led crusades, inquisitions, pogroms, imperialistic conquests, slavery, recent wars, and holocausts. We have used Bible verses to justify all of it. We listened to Christian leaders who told us it was the godly thing to do. And although there have always been believers who resisted these shameful movements, far too many Christians accepted the hate and wasted resources on spreading that twisted version of the good news.

We've preached "Jesus is the answer," but lived like He's not.

So I'm praying for our generation.

For us to have a different response.

Try a different method (which is in actual fact the original method).

Right now, it feels like the world's system is asking for a new religious war. The grumblings are in the air, yet the only thing we followers of Christ should be fighting is the temptation of "us vs. them," "Christian vs. Muslim," "*Allahu Akbar* vs. God is great." I'm not saying Islam is correct, I'm just saying that I want to focus on the ways in which I believe Christianity is right.

How do American followers of Jesus respond to the escalation of hatred and violence? What are we to do if Muslims begin to be targeted and registered in the US? What would Jesus do if He lived in America in the twenty-first century? Show love and teach peace. Stand up for religious liberty. And then actually serve and engage our Muslim friends and enemies.

As my good friend, the great theologian Bob Ekblad wrote,

> When James and John ask Jesus if they should call down fire from heaven to consume the Samaritans, Jesus rebukes them, saying: "You do not know of what spirit you are of. For the son of man did not come to destroy men's lives but to save them" (Luke 9:55–56).

Those following Jesus need empowerment by the Holy Spirit to love our neighbors, to love our enemies, and to actively pursue understanding and reconciliation. This includes first taking the log out of our own eyes through confessing our sin and renouncing our violence and hate. We must refuse our natural proclivity to judge the other, and to seek instead understanding with anyone we label an "offender."[3]

I have met many Muslims, and almost every one of them has opened up their hearts toward me in relationship and hospitality. Every month I intentionally take part in a Muslim-Christian fellowship meal. Sometimes it is inside a mosque. Other times inside a church. But every time I go, I sense the pleasure of God. Sure, we think differently about salvation and the world, and I'm persuaded to show them the ways of Christ, but I do it convinced that God loves them as much as He loves me.

Jesus does not prefer Christians over Muslims.

Jesus does not love believers more than He loves non-believers.

We are not called to be pro-Christian, but rather Christ-like.

So, as a Christian pastor, I renounce Islamophobia and choose again the master plan of the wonderful Counselor.

Fear will not choose how I love.

The Sermon on the Mount already did that.

Notes

1. Carl Medearis, *Simple Ways to Reach Out to Muslims* (Bloomington, MN: Bethany House, 2008), ebook.
2. Nathan Hamm, Twitter post, November 15, 2015, 2:37 p.m., http://twitter.com/NathanHamm.
3. Bob Ekbad, "I am Not Charlie: a Christian response to the killings in Paris," *Bob & Gracie Ekblad* (blog), January 12, 2015, http://www.bobekblad.com/i-am-not-charlie-a-christian-response-to-the-killings-in-paris/. (Accessed March 27, 2017.)

40

DRAW THE LINE SOMEWHERE

"To be a Christian means to forgive the inexcusable in others,
because God has forgiven the inexcusable in you."[1]
—*C. S. Lewis*

Jesus loves the people we hate, so here's a humongous "what if?" What if our loudest response to terrorism at home is mercy abroad? What if the way to be done with mass shootings would be to declare mass forgiveness? What if we stood with the broken, hurting people of the Middle East as we stand with the broken, hurting people of the Western world? What if, instead of investing all that money in politics and war, we "invaded" each of our "enemy" nations and used that money to build shelters and schools, clean water sources and clinics? I believe in answering these "what if's?" with the New Testament strategy:

1. *"Do not resist the one who is evil. But if anyone slaps you on the right cheek, turn to him the other also"* —Jesus (Matthew 5:39).

2. *"Do not be overcome by evil, but overcome evil with good"* —Paul (Romans 12:21).

3. *"The anger of man does not produce the righteousness of God"* —James (James 1:20).

The New Testament gives us enough material to go on and on and on. You see, the only way to defeat radical Islamic terrorism or radical fundamentalism in Christianity (or any other kind of radical extremism) is to love radically. And the gospel (our manifesto and constitution) is full of this kind of radical love.

The New Testament was written in a time when believers were being persecuted and martyred, when their surroundings were chaotic and their lives were in danger—every...single...day.

They too had valid reasons to hate and retaliate. These first-century Christians were losing their homes, their children, and their peace. They were surrounded by religious terrorists who murdered them, and political terrorists who persecuted them. However, they went in the opposite direction; they resisted the temptation to use Satan's tools. They demonstrated forgiveness and compassion, even when hatred and war would have been an appropriate response.

They modeled their Messiah, not Rome.

You see, Saul of Tarsus was a terrorist. Before his miraculous conversion, the writer of more than 40 percent of the New Testament was a kind of Al-Qaeda or ISIS of sorts. The first Christian martyrdom happened under his authority. The victim was Stephen, a young man whose only crime was preaching Jesus. His "just" reward was lawful murder (stuck inside a hole, while rocks disfigured his head).

Terrifying.

Nonetheless, when Stephen was breathing his last breath, he asked God to forgive the ones who were killing him. He prayed, while being mutilated to death, *"Lord, do not hold this sin against them."*[2]

The Father heard that prayer, was pleased with it, and answered it by revealing himself to Saul the commander of the stone throwers. He is now and forever the apostle Paul.

Terrific.

If somehow this chapter sounds ridiculous to you...well, welcome to my world! Whenever terrorist attacks happen, I think of my own family and all I want is to protect them at all cost—from radicalism and every other evil. But the way of the cross is an absolute contradiction to human nature (it's part of our new nature as new creation). That's why the Bible says to *"regard no one according to the flesh,"*[3] because Jesus does not see our enemies as His enemies, and His body on a cross was God's love letter to them.

If we think that the words of Jesus apply to individuals but not to nations, then we should just call him a "life-coach," not King and Savior.

So I ask again, what would jihadists experience if we Christians took Christ literally? *"Do good to those who hate you, bless those who curse you, pray for those who abuse you."*[4]

Jesus said it about the cruel Roman Empire of His time, as much as He's saying it about the evil ISIS of ours.

Yes, let's continue to pray for the victims and their families. Let's bless our governments to respond with wisdom. Let's stand with the communities affected in these times of grief and sadness. Support organizations that attend to the persecuted church. And let's pray for our Muslim friends around the world.

As the first martyr of our faith prayed, we unanimously say: *"Lord, do not hold this sin against them!"*

Notes

1. C. S. Lewis, *The Weight of Glory* (New York: HarperCollins Publishing, 1976), 182.
2. Acts 7:60.
3. 2 Corinthians 5:16.
4. Luke 6:27–28.

41

BEING PROPERLY PRO

"There are three stages to every great work of God; first it is impossible, then it is difficult, then it is done."[1]
—*James Hudson Taylor*

It would be the greatest "problem" in our nation's history. All 664,435 unwanted babies, alive-not-aborted, and ready to be loved. That's how many abortions were performed in America in 2013.

Dear church, are you ready to take them in?

I like what Smith Wigglesworth used to say, "The Book of Acts was written, only because the apostles acted."[2]

Every election cycle seems to highlight the important conversation between pro-life and pro-choice. But this chapter has nothing to do with what a politician could do (because politicians come and go), this is an invitation to the body of Christ…way beyond what happens in our elections or outside of them.

If we want to stop abortion, then we need to fully embrace adoption. Not the theory but the practice. It costs roughly four hundred dollars for an abortion, and forty thousand-plus dollars for an adoption.

Dear church, are we ready to invest?

If we want to defund Planned Parenthood, we need to take responsibility for all of the other helpful services it provides to low income families. If we want to call ourselves *pro-life* then we need to be *pro-everyone's lives*—those in the womb, the ones in Syria, and the ones in our prison system. Our compassion cannot terminate after nine months. If it does, then we should label ourselves "pro-birth," and after birth, label ourselves "pro-me."

Yes, abortion is evil! And I wish I could use another adjective, something less insulting to the readers who are okay with it, but as a father of two I can't find another word to describe the choice of stopping the noise. Hearing the sound of my sons' heartbeats was the most beautiful music I have ever heard; the rhythm and speed made my heart dance differently. It was like I heard God singing, and from that moment onward, everything in me embraced the privilege of being a father.

Twenty-two days after conception, my babies' hearts were pumping. Pumping.

And it's hard to think that in the land in which we live, it is both legal and profitable to turn off that music. As Mahatma Gandhi said, "It seems to me as clear as daylight that abortion would be a crime."[3]

Yet in the midst of my righteous anger, I have to remember that Jesus died for them too, and still loves them perfectly. Jesus is pro-*their* life. No doubt that God fearfully and wonderfully made every woman who has gone through an abortion, every man who has pushed for one, and every one of us who judged them for it.

So my response has to come from outside of myself.

My opinions won't change anything; I have to take the God approach.

I don't want to be the pastor/father/author who just talks about what is wrong or right or left or Christ. I don't want to be pushing my values on others while turning such huge issues into nine-hundred-word articles for Facebook and HappySonship.com. Yes, my natural reaction is to be angry, to point the finger, and to have a call to action against these acts (and there is a proper place for that).

But more than anything, I want to overwhelm the malicious with the wonderful.

That's how Jesus did it.

That's the grace agenda.

That will change the world.

The great Brennan Manning said it like this:

The danger of the pro-life position, which I vigorously support, is
that it can be frighteningly selective. The rights of the unborn and
the dignity of the age-worn are pieces of the same pro-life fabric.
We weep at the unjustified destruction of the unborn. Did we also
weep when the evening news reported from Arkansas that a black
family had been shotgunned out of a white neighborhood? When
we laud life and blast abortionists, our credibility as Christians is
questionable. On one hand we proclaim the love and anguish, the
pain and joy that goes into fashioning a single child. We proclaim
how precious each life is to God and should be to us. On the other
hand, when it is the enemy that shrieks to heaven with his flesh in
flames, we do not weep, we are not shamed; we call for more.[4]

I believe it's our right to speak up. Our understanding of abortion as
murder has a place in the national discourse. However, it's time for the
church to embrace the ultimate call in this pro-life/pro-choice debate:

Adoption.

Seeing the issue as if there are no unwanted children, just unfound
families.

Catherine and I have been on an adoption journey for the last five years.
It has been a whirlwind of emotions that has cost thousands of dollars and
huge amounts of time and energy. There is still so much to be done. And
a lot of times we felt like giving up, but we find no other place in God that
feels as real and as good (and as worth it).

We also have to understand that different situations bring a woman
to an abortion center. Every would-be mom has a story that needs to be
heard. We shouldn't expect them to choose life because we throw them
Bible verses and "motivate" them with our morality.

Our votes won't change their hearts.

Our way is adoption.

Our method is love.

And with them, we can make abortion obsolete.

Let's be the answer every time there is an unwanted pregnancy. Amy Ford and Embrace Grace helps when they want to keep the baby, and you can be the solution when they don't.

Also, our generation needs to talk openly about sex, abstinence, and birth control; we faith leaders need to be less concerned with preaching the law and more intentional about living the gospel in these times and for this generation. We should put our money and resources into homes and adoption grants and give legitimate assistant to people who are foster parents.

I believe that in our time we will see every Planned Parenthood center full of believers who are ready to help, assist, adopt, care, and love...both the godly inside the womb and the godly outside of it.

Are you ready to open your home to one of the 664,435?

We're due for the book of Acts 2.0.

Notes

1. Quoted in Leslie T. Lyall, *A Passion for the Impossible* (London: OMF Books, 1965), 5.
2. Smith Wigglesworth, *Smith Wigglesworth Devotional* (New Kensington, PA: Whitaker House, 1999), 18.
3. M. K. Gandhi, *Self Restraint v. Self Indulgence* (Ahmedabad, India: Nabu Press, 1947), 156.
4. Brennan Manning, *The Ragamuffin Gospel: Good News for the Bedraggled, Beat-Up, and Burnt Out* (Colorado Springs: Multnomah Books, 2008), 136.

42

WHO IS HE...REALLY?

"The Lord is not slow to fulfill his promise as some count slowness, but is patient toward you, not wishing that any should perish, but that all should reach repentance."[1]
—*Apostle Peter*

Abba. Savior. King. Master. Friend...on and on we could go. Yet ultimately, and I can say this confidently as a new covenant Bible-believing Christian leader, God *is* love. His very nature and essence is love. His driving force and motivation is love. And the way he acts and reacts are the manifestations of His perfect love for us.

Every other filter used to explain God (outside of love) is a filter that needs the love of God. Now, you've probably figured this out while reading this book, but I'm still trying to figure things out. My best theological response for most things is: "I don't know." However, there is one certainty in my life, the one definite I can build my family and my ministry upon: His name is Jesus, and Jesus *is* love.

The family of Father, Son, and Holy Spirit has included us into this eternal display of affection and honor. Not just the language of it, but its full experience.

And the wonderful thing is that Jesus did not come to earth just to validate the information that *God is love*…He came to manifest it fully. And we are its glorious display.

When the teachers judge, Jesus welcomes. When the Pharisees condemn, Jesus forgives. When the scribes reject, Jesus heals. If this is not the Christ we serve, then stop calling me a Christian.

Also, this Jesus enjoys going to the strip club. And I know this to be true because my friend Rochelle goes in there with Him. She used to be a stripper herself. Drugs, abuse, and the need to be loved pushed her to the place where stripping seemed to be her only choice. She danced for men; she wept for freedom; she encountered Christ.

Now Rochelle leads Lipstick Ministries. They go to strip clubs in North Carolina and hand-deliver bags of lipstick, toiletries, and other feminine products to the dancers. They provide words of encouragement to the dancers just before they go on stage. They pray for the dancers' children, for their families, and for their futures. They go into strip clubs and erotic massage parlors, fully loaded with the love of God, and with that love (and their own testimony of freedom) they give the dancers hope.

They have countless testimonies of lives changed. And they do it by revealing (through tenderness and action) the Christ of John 8. We have countless reasons to judge these woman…and one reason alone to not: Jesus Himself—His example, His invitation, His gospel of love.

I need radical examples of love like this because I have a tendency to be more pharisaical than Christlike. I've developed a new spiritual discipline that I want to share with you. It's called stone-dropping. Whenever my brain enters into judgmental overdrive I picture myself grabbing all those thoughts (stones) from my mind and releasing them outside of myself. I literally act it out. I take my right hand, do a sweeping motion over my head (as if I am picking up stones from the floor), and then I extend my hand away from me and I release my tight grip (releasing all those stones from my grasp).

I do this throughout the day, while I'm driving into work, while I'm watching the news, while listening to prayers I disagree with, and while worshipping at church and assuming the worst about the worshippers around me. I do it because I am aware that my weakness is to complain and compare. I do it because I want to remind my flesh that Christ in me is not a judgmental legalist, but rather a Lover of people. He is the One who sees things as they truly are and declares value and worth over everyone He both agrees and disagrees with.

According to Scripture, whoever is united with the Lord is one with Him in spirit.[2]

That's the miracle of this invitation. It's the possibility that judgment and gossip can become a reminder of His mercy and compassion. And if you allow the real you to come out, the you that is one with the Savior, then the hurts and the pains that you carry will have the potential to become streams of healing and the beginning of a love reformation.

Remember, not judging is actually judging rightly. Not judging is admitting to yourself that you are not perfect, and yet, you are perfectly loved (and so are they).

You should try it. Take your throwing hand and use your imagination to collect all those stones, and then drop them as seeds of grace.

Or not.

Either way, I won't judge.

Notes

1. 2 Peter 3:9 esv.
2. 1 Corinthians 6:17.

43

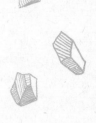

DOUBLE GIFT

"The future is dark. But my faith dares me to ask:
What if this darkness is not darkness of the tomb,
but darkness of the womb?"[1]
—*Valarie Kaur*

I left this chapter to the very end, not because it's at the end of the book, but more so because I've been waiting for this story to have a happy ending. Today is the deadline for this manuscript to be delivered—and we still have not heard about finalizing our adoption.

At three weeks old she was abandoned, a gift despised, sweet and pure yet familiar with the ways of rejection. Our collective sinful nature created an environment in which a twenty-one-day-old baby has no home. And she's just of one of the sixty million orphans alive in the world today.

No parents, no comfort, no hope—just a name in a system, another sad statistic, a few details here and there. Yet, as soon as we heard *her* name, we said *yes*.

Sitota.

It's the Amharic word for *gift*, and she's our precious daughter in waiting.

Our dream come true, our joy in Ethiopia.

You know I've been a fraud. Something in me has always wanted to do good works in order to balance my sinful nature. I wanted to feel holier than others. My insecurities drove me to preach more, write more, and "sin" less. I wanted to plan an adoption so I could compare myself with others and be found superior. Somehow, I wanted to prove to the world that I was a real Christian. A *better* Christian.

And I was so hungry for a story that shouted, "Carlos is so awesome!" I yearned for social media to watch and celebrate us as "the Puerto Rican-British couple who adopted a baby girl from Ethiopia, have two gorgeous boys, and won the Cutest-Family-in-the-World Award."

But now I know her name.

Sitota.

And I couldn't care less about anything else. My heart is undone for the girl I will walk down the aisle someday. She is no longer an idea, no longer a statement to my "holiness." She's a living, breathing, darling woman. Born to be loved, here to be accepted, and ours to be included.

I want her playing with her brothers, eating my rice and beans, dancing with her mom, and worshiping at our church.

Psalm 68:5 says, *"Father of the fatherless and protector of widows is God in his holy habitation."* In His private room in the heavens, Abba Father's main job is to protect my baby girl.

My tears for her have joy inside, yet they are also drenched with pain. Our case worker at the adoption agency is currently in Ethiopia, so my insomnia carries excitement, although worry is tied with it. A few months back, Catherine and I watched a documentary on Netflix called *The Drop Box.* It tells the story of South Korean pastor Lee Jong-rak and his heroic efforts to save newborns. It is a heart-wrenching observation of the physical, emotional, and financial toll associated with providing refuge to orphans that would otherwise be abandoned on the streets. Pastor Lee has saved hundreds of babies and adopted the ones that no one else wanted. I was in a downpour from minute five until the very end of the credits.

Yes, *The Drop Box* is a true story of hope—a reminder that every human life is sacred and worthy of love. But now I want it to be my story.

I'm tired of watching movies that move me. I'm done with hearing sermons about changing the world. My life is sold out for God's dream in Sitota.

I hope that you've felt frustration while reading this book—frustration against injustice, poverty, religion, anything! As Graham Cooke likes to say, "Working with frustration is the key in turning our potential into something actual. Most people are frustrated because they care about something. They must allow the Holy Spirit to direct that frustration into something meaningful."[2]

Yes, my dear friend, whatever frustrates you the most, you were probably born to change.

For Catherine and me, it's hunger and orphanhood. So we're asking God for the empowerment to do something about it, and adopting Sitota has been the product of our frustration with sin becoming an invitation to change.

Isabela is the name of the town in Puerto Rico where we were married. We always wanted to give our daughter that name. To send a message to her heart that her story began the day we began ours.

The name Isabela also means gift. *Gift of God.*

Our daughter. Our opportunity. Our double gift.

This adoption process has been challenging. It has created a number of concerns about money, parenting, and family dynamics. But our love for Isabela Sitota Rodríguez Roberts arrived instantly.

And at the end of the day, *"the greatest of these is love."*[3]

I believe with all of my heart that by the time you are reading these lines, darling girl will be reading them too; here at home with her family, where she belongs, where she will learn to drop the stones. Here, she will be challenged to forgive the ones who abandoned her, to respect the ones who make fun of her, and to follow Jesus, even if it costs her everything.

Her right will be to choose whether she believes it and lives it.

Just like you.

We're almost at the end of our journey together. Only a few extra pages remain.

What are you going to choose?

When you're the woman caught in the act of adultery, will you choose to listen to the grace of Christ and then go and sin no more?

When you're tempted to stone and judge, will you choose to surrender your self-righteousness for the beautiful journey of humility and servanthood?

And when you're invited again to follow the ways of the Word, will you be *Him* to the broken and the hurting?

Such a big decision.

Yet such an easy choice.

Notes

1. Valerie Kaur, "A Sikh prayer for America on November 9th, 2016," *Valleric Kaur: storytelling for social change* (blog), November 11, 2016, http://valariekaur.com/2016/11/a-sikh-prayer-for-america-on-november-9th-2016/. (Accessed March 28, 2017.)
2. Graham Cooke, *A Divine Confrontation* (Shippensburg, PA: Destiny Image Publishers, 1999), 301.
3. 1 Corinthians 13:13.

ACT 4

THE READER

Jesus is still looking at you as the woman who was caught in the act of adultery leaves the temple, in love and completely free. She keeps looking back to Jesus and singing in a loud enough voice, *"Set me as a seal upon your heart, as a seal upon your arm, for love is strong as death...."*[1]

And there was no doubt in her heart that the hero who liberated her is the Christ who saves you. Yes, she's surprised to see you walk by. "How are you here?" she asks. But she knows, without you answering, that you had to come see Him.

And you look like one of His.

You bring your pain and baggage. You carry it like a sack of potatoes or a cross made of steel. You approach Him carefully with excitement. "My sheep hear my voice," He says to you, and that is when your heart begins to explode. Slowly, fiercely.

In the presence of such compassion there is no need to hide your worst, so boldly you share your heart with Him. He smiles as you talk. He reaches His fingers to catch your tears. He is everything you've been looking for.

As you speak, you catch the writings of Jesus on the floor. You look at Him astonished, and you smile as you notice all 667 words scrawled on the ground. He nods rapidly with a grin and says, "Yes, now you know." You also notice that all the stones dropped by the Pharisees and teachers of the law are still on the ground. They're lined up as tombstones, like a graveyard for religion. Joy fills your hearts and you begin to laugh with the Christ.

Still, you feel your knuckles tighten and realize that there is one rock left in your hand. You were keeping it just in case; maybe to use on yourself, maybe on your spouse, maybe a politician, a pastor, or a friend. *You never know.* And even though you are sitting next to Jesus, it is still hard to let it go.

But He grabs it from your hand and drops it on His toe.

He bites the side of His bottom lip, closes His eyes tight, and after a slow groan, says, "Ouch."

You both laugh together again.

Again and again.

You experience the presence where there is fullness of joy. Right there at His right hand is pleasure forevermore. And you feel that so truly and deeply, that you decide to stay there. No one is taking you away from this temple, this holy ground, this special day.

Jesus looks straight into your eyes and says, "Take up your cross and follow me."

You don't even hesitate.

You say yes immediately.

And off you go, together with the King, alive and in love, and with no stones in sight.

Notes

1. Song of Solomon 8:6.

EPILOGUE

"Having heard all of this,
you may choose to look the other way but you can
never again say you did not know."[1]
—*William Wilberforce*

William Wilberforce was the leader of the anti-slavery movement in England. He met Jesus, believed the words of Jesus, and decided to walk in the Jesus way. His work stopped the abusive trading of human beings from Africa to the New World. And now it's your turn.

I know that I could not cover the many important justice issues that require our attention and our action. Human trafficking, the rejection of refugees, and extreme poverty are three of the many pains our world is still plagued with. Yet *you* are the anointed. You prayed it out loud in chapter 25. Now it's time to live it. And as the Bible says, "*The whole law is fulfilled in one word: 'You shall love your neighbor as yourself.'*"[2]

Go find the need, be the friend, feed the hungry, hug the homeless, call the politicians who represent you, welcome a stranger, and hang out with the worst. You don't *have* to do it, but you *get* to do it, and I know that Jesus is waiting for you there.

In this social media world, there is no reason for us not stay connected. So use @HappySonship in Twitter, Pinterest, or Instagram (or any of the other platforms) and tell me how it's going.

Also visit TheHappyGivers.com store, where every cent you spend will be used in our children's home in Peru (Casa de Paz), our ministry to inmates in the US prison system (Inside Hope), and/or our ministry to help families fund their adoption process (Project Next).

You can also join The Happy Givers team on one of our international mission trips. Come with me and let's discover together how we can help others to become empowered, funded, and loved.

That would be fun!

I love you.

I believe in you.

Hasta luego.

Endnotes

1. Close of a speech in House of Commons (1791), as quoted in Kay Marshall Storm, *Once Blind: The Life of John Newton* (Colorado Springs: Authentic Publishing, 2007), 225.
2. Galatians 5:14.

ACKNOWLEDGMENTS

Mami y Papi, gracias por creer en mi, gracias por amarme aun en la distancia y gracias por darme tanto espacio para encontrar a Dios. Los amo.

Catherine Rachel Roberts, the easiest part about writing this book was dedicating it to you. My heart is truly amazed at your capacity for grace. I cherish every moment with you. And I'm so proud to be your one and only. Te amo chichi.

Alejandro and Sebastián, you boys are the most glorious sons a dad could ever have. I'm grateful to God for the privilege of discovering you every day. You want to wrestle later?

Isabela Sitota, you will never know how much you mean to me, my Ethiopian princess. You are my favorite gift and I cannot wait to have you in my arms…ē wĕd shä′ lō.

To mom and dad and my sisters in England, I love you more than I show it.

To my sisters in Puerto Rico, *son las mejores. Besos y abrazos.*

Don Milan, for becoming a friend through this process. Your push and encouragement were essential.

To Duncan and Kate, John and Carol, Murray and Ash, and my whole family at Catch the Fire around the world, you should all be named in this page. But I ain't doing that. Just know that I love you and I believe in our movement.

To the team at Whitaker House—Bob Whitaker, Christine Whitaker, Tom Cox, Cathy Hickling, and Jim Armstrong. An amazing crew with amazing integrity. Huge thank you!

To Abel, for pushing me to write. To Puddle, for pushing me to publish. To Sven and Eli, for being friends and fans. To Lisa and Elius, *por ser mi famila*. To Kristen, Yuki, and Paola, for being the top three (ever).

Finally, to all the heroes who gave me endorsements, I owe you all a big plate of rice and beans, with plantains and avocado and a Chilean red.

Lastly (and most importantly) to the living God above, who continually gives me His majestic love. I am forever indebted to You, Jesus, and I can't wait to spend eternity at Your feet, surrendering my crowns and saying, "Thank You for not stoning me (or anyone else who ever lived). You're amazing!"

ABOUT THE AUTHOR

Carlos is passionate about reaching the world with God's radical love. He is a provocative preacher, pastor, teacher, and blogger who serves the local church and loves to be among prisoners, young adults, and anyone who dares to think differently. For fifteen years he has been traveling the world reaching the most broken people with hugs, passion, and the stories in Luke 15. Founding pastor of Catch the Fire in Raleigh, NC, Carlos has written several articles for *Relevant* and *Revival* magazines and published his first book *Simple Sonship* in 2014. Also in 2014, he began HappySonship.com, an online magazine that reaches thousands of people daily by sharing the message of grace via whatever the heck is trending on the web. The website has now become an international nonprofit focusing on empowering children in Peru, reconnecting families with inmates in the US prison system, and helping parents fund their adoption process. Carlos and (his British darling) Catherine have two gorgeous boys and are awaiting a baby girl through adoption.

Oh yeah, he also wants everyone to know that he's a Puerto Rican and he can't wait to tell you all about it.

HappySonship.com

SchoolofRevival.com

TheHappyGivers.com